Staffordshire Library and Information Service

Please return or renew or by the last date shown

If not required by other readers, this item may be renewed
in person, by post or telephone, online or by email.
To renew, either the book or ticket are required

**24 Hour Renewal Line
0845 33 00 740**

Staffordshire
County Council

D0272835

Secrets of a German PoW

To my daughter April,
for her unfailing love and support

Secrets of a German PoW

The Revelations of Hauptmann Herbert Cleff

Brian Brinkworth

O what a tangled web we weave
When first we practise to deceive!
Sir Walter Scott, *Marmion*, 1808

Pen & Sword
AVIATION

First published in Great Britain in 2014 by
Pen & Sword Aviation
an imprint of
Pen & Sword Books Ltd
47 Church Street
Barnsley
South Yorkshire
S70 2AS

ISBN 978 1 78303 295 2

A CIP catalogue record for this book is available from the British
Library

Typeset in Ehrhardt by
Mac Style, Bridlington, East Yorkshire
Printed and bound in the UK by CPI Group (UK) Ltd,
Croydon, CRO 4YY

Pen & Sword Books Ltd incorporates the imprints of Pen &
Sword Archaeology, Atlas, Aviation, Battleground, Discovery,
Family History, History, Maritime, Military, Naval, Politics,
Railways, Select, Transport, True Crime, and Fiction, Frontline
Books, Leo Cooper, Praetorian Press, Seaforth Publishing and
Wharncliffe.

For a complete list of Pen & Sword titles please contact
PEN & SWORD BOOKS LIMITED
47 Church Street, Barnsley, South Yorkshire, S70 2AS, England
E-mail: enquiries@pen-and-sword.co.uk
Website: www.pen-and-sword.co.uk

Contents

List of Illustrations

Author's Preface

I came upon this story obliquely. It arose from a study that I had made of the Miles M.52, the first aircraft to be designed to fly supersonically. This had been ordered by the Ministry of Aircraft Production in 1943, with a requirement to reach a maximum speed of 1,000mph in level flight. That was substantially more than twice the speed of the frontline fighter aircraft in service at the time. The order had been placed on a small firm, where the mere handful of men who could be spared for this extraordinary task quickly sized up what would be needed for flight in conditions that had never been experienced before. They produced a design that later became justly famous in aeronautical circles. It was well suited to the requirement, in many ways reflecting a level of understanding that would not be matched generally for a decade. My interest was in trying to find out how the designers had gone about this job, in relation to the state of knowledge at the time. The outcome was a paper published by the Royal Aeronautical Society[*].

Only the most critical of situations could have called up so ambitious a project, in the middle of the Second World War, at a time when virtually all of British industrial capacity was at full stretch in a struggle for the country's very survival. The few records about it that had been found subsequently reported that it had been started because a Prisoner of War had claimed that aircraft with

---

[*] Brinkworth B J, On the aerodynamics of the Miles M.52 (E.24/43) – a historical perspective. The Aeronautical Journal of the Royal Aeronautical Society, Vol 114, No 1153, March 2010, pp125–156.

comparable performance had already been developed in Germany. It was enough that the enemy might have made a spectacular technical advance, in an aspect of aeronautics that the Allies had neglected almost completely. But amid a collection of speculations that had gathered around this project later it was said that it had all been a mistake – that the prisoner had reported a speed of 1,000 kilometres per hour, and this had been miss-typed as 1,000 miles per hour.

The Germans had indeed reached 1,000kph, but that was not a supersonic speed. From the papers that I had reviewed for my study, it was clear that there had been no such mistake. In the course of his interrogation, it had been pointed out to the prisoner that the speeds he reported were well into the supersonic range, and he agreed that they were, adding some comments on the different design of wings that were required for operation in that new regime.

Full records of the original interrogations that had set the matter in motion were not filed with the minutes of the meetings at which they had been discussed and acted upon, nor had the prisoner's identity been disclosed there. I began to wonder if it would be possible to find more, although there was no clear starting-point, and in any case it was likely that the records from 1942–3 would not have survived. But after a considerable amount of what my daughter described as 'archivology', they were at length uncovered. What they revealed began a wider quest to find out all that I could about the man, which eventually extended in effect from cradle to grave. He proved to have had a remarkable life, with the strikingly unexpected ramifications that are the subject of this book. Being a German Prisoner-of-War, who in 1943 found himself living freely in London and commuting daily to a job in Whitehall, was just one of these.

I have had to make some decisions about nomenclature here. Our man was a junior officer when he was captured, and I have rendered his rank of *Hauptmann* as 'Captain', the nearest British equivalent.

There were many different versions of the rank of *General* in the German army, but where any holders of these are named, I have called them simply 'General'. Wherever German words are to be quoted, especially technical terms, the English equivalent is given. Other terms and units usually remain as used at the time. In the British documentation, the term Prisoner-of-War was abbreviated to 'P/W', becoming the version 'PoW' that we know today only in the later stages of the war, but I have used the latter throughout, except where an extract using the former is being quoted directly. Security classifications are cited as they were given at the time; for example, the highest British classification was Most Secret, being replaced by Top Secret later, when a new uniform nomenclature was adopted jointly by the Allies.

A list of the principal sources on which I have drawn is given between the end of the text and the Index. I thank most warmly the many individuals and persons in organisations who have generously provided information and/or allowed extracts from printed works to be quoted, and these contributors are acknowledged there also.

Brian Brinkworth,
Hampshire, 2013

Chapter One

M 164

1.1 Capture

By the beginning of November 1942, British and Commonwealth forces of the 8th Army in Egypt had fought a costly advance westward along the Mediterranean coast from El Alamein. The opposing German and Italian forces, depleted in men and materials and short of fuel, were preparing to make a withdrawal into Libya. But, directed by an order from Hitler to hold their position, they suffered further losses without being able to halt the advance. The tanks of the 21st *Panzer Division* were severely mauled. On 4 November, their commander, General Wilhelm Ritter von Thoma, was captured in the field and on 6 November, the Headquarters of the *Panzer Armee* near El Dab'a were overrun. Amongst those taken prisoner there was Herbert Cleff, in Panzer field uniform, with the rank of Captain. Although at first tagged only by a bland Prisoner-of-War reference number, he soon came to the attention of senior intelligence officers, which would lead to his transfer to Britain, with altogether remarkable consequences.

Cleff held the title of *Technischer Kriegsverwaltungsrat*, initially translated (roughly) to be Technical Staff Administrative Officer. Someone holding a post of that description might not normally have attracted much interest. The reference to administration in the title could have indicated that Cleff acted in some executive capacity, perhaps in the equivalent of the Adjutant's office. But he had stated that he had arrived in Libya recently by being flown 'directly from Stalingrad', where some of the fiercest fighting on the German Eastern Front was raging, so it was perhaps thought that he might have some inside knowledge of that. He was taken to the Middle East branch of the Combined Services Detailed Interrogation Centre (CSDIC, ME) in Cairo, now with the reference number M164, to see whether any useful information might be obtained from him. This would take place routinely by the usual methods of British interrogation, keeping it at a conversational level with people of similar rank, including, in the terms of the first report issued about him, by 'the Interrogating Officer becoming his pupil pro.tem., an almost infallible trick with intelligent Germans'. Information was gained there also by the use of 'stool-pigeons', disillusioned prisoners who had agreed to talk with newcomers and report back what had been learned from them.

At first, Cleff refused to give any details of his work, deflecting questions firmly though politely. But in contrast, he had been forthcoming about his personal history and the theatres in which he had served, from which a picture began to emerge. His first involvement with the military had been as a civilian engineer in the Army's weapons development organisation. In this capacity he had accompanied the German forces during the invasion of Poland, but in November 1939 he was called up into the Army, despite a low medical category, said to be due to 'poor physique, weak eyesight and rheumatic heart trouble'. After perfunctory military training (chiefly in saluting), during 1940 he accompanied Rommel's Ghost Division of tanks in the western advance through Holland and Belgium and subsequent operations in France. He was promoted to the rank of Captain, in the 'silverfish' division (in full dress, as shown in Fig 1, his jacket would have had silver rather than the usual pink piping of the Panzer uniform). It was learnt from him later that the award of the Iron Cross, of which he is wearing the ribbon at the second button-hole, had been for his work in the French campaign. At some point he was lucky not to have been killed in a tank, when a shell penetrated the armour close to his head. He appears to be wearing the cross itself on his breast pocket, which would indicate that his award was raised to First Class at some point.

From June 1941, he had taken part in the Russian 'Eastern Campaign', at first under General Heinz Guderian in Army Group Centre. His report of having crossed the River Bug in an amphibious tank, and mention of actions at Bialystok, Brest-Litovsk, Minsk, Smolensk and the Moscow area, were consistent with his having been with the 2nd Panzer Group. At some point he had been detached to operations in Yugoslavia. He said that latterly he had been involved in the south-eastward advance of Army Group South through the Ukraine, with Feodosiya and Sevastopol in the Crimea being mentioned, and then via Kharkov and Rostov to Stalingrad. These somewhat erratic movements were however typical of the hasty redeployment of German resources over great distances at this stage of the Russian campaign. He might not have known at that point how hugely fortunate he was to have been directed out of the Stalingrad sector. Very soon afterwards, this was to be termed the 'Cauldron', in which the German 6th Army was irretrievably confined after being encircled by Soviet forces from 22 November. What followed there was a conflict regarded as the most bloody in the history of warfare, with total casualties on all sides variously estimated to be up to two million. The remnant of the German army was finally overcome with its commander, Field Marshall Friedrich von Paulus, amongst those taken prisoner.

Although having reported the outline of his personal experiences with more than usual detail, Cleff had still been refusing to answer direct questions about his work. But during the informal conversations he began to voice his opinions about things such as the relative merits of the tanks fielded by the Axis and Allied powers. The level of detail in these comments showed that, far from being involved in routine administration, he was in fact an expert in tank engineering. Once this had become clear, he was more forthcoming. His role had been to observe and record the effectiveness of design features of tanks under battle conditions in different theatres of operation. Although he had acted as a civilian in government service before the war, after the formal declaration of hostilities he had been called up, despite being medically unfit. There is no evidence of any intention that he should engage in fighting; instead this formal absorption into the army was perhaps necessary in order to ensure that, if he were captured, being in uniform he would be protected under the provisions of the Geneva Convention from the risk of being executed as a spy. It could also have been hoped that the vagueness of the title allocated to him might deflect interest away from his real occupation.

There is already more than a suggestion here that his capabilities had been well regarded in the German Army. In Egypt, his task was to be an observer of technical aspects of operating tanks in desert conditions, in the course of which he claimed to have visited all the German tank units in the North African Theatre, and to have had frequent interviews with the commander of the Afrika Korps, Field Marshal Erwin Rommel.

1.2 Army interrogation 1

There is a sense here that Cleff wanted his experience and knowledge of his field to be respected by his interrogators. Even with someone not overtly boastful, this carries a risk. Concerning technical matters, he seemed careful to refer only to things that he might reasonably expect to be already known, but the extent of that could never be certain. And so, amongst things of little consequence, hints were obtained that might have been useful when taken in conjunction with information from others. A measure of the interest in Cleff is that, over the next three months, seventeen verbatim accounts of his interrogations in Cairo were recorded in the 'S.R.' series of documents. They were summarised in two CSDIC reports, Army 1361 and 1836, totalling nine foolscap pages, which showed the wide scope of his remarks about aspects of tank engineering

Some of these were expressions of Cleff's own opinions about the process of tank design. Ideally, he thought, this would be a systematic procedure, in which all aspects of the requirements for a fighting vehicle in foreseeable circumstances were first established. Next, early layouts of machines to meet these requirements would be realised in one or more trial designs, and experimental prototypes would be built and field tested, which would often reveal factors which had not been anticipated. Only then could the detailed design and preparation for manufacture begin. There should be an opportunity to follow this process in peacetime, but often it had not been managed well. In war, it was now overtaken by the urgency to respond to technical developments by the opposing forces. He recognised that through haste, mistakes had been made by all the present combatants – German, British, American and Russian (he was more generally dismissive of Italian and French tanks, making few references to those). Concerning hull design, he instanced the early American medium tanks, which had a heavy gun mounted towards one side of the hull, as well as a turret with a lighter one. Their high profile had made them vulnerable in action, and the interior layout was uncomfortable for the crew and hindered them in their tasks. What is today called the ergonomics had not been sufficiently considered. This lesson had been learnt for the design of the American M4 Sherman tank, which Cleff considered to be the best all-round tank in the Theatre at the time.

British tanks had been hampered by the decision to use engines that were already in existence for other purposes, particularly those originally designed for aircraft. These were not sufficiently robust to withstand the severe and incessant jolting experienced in tank operations. British tanks had been sent as aid to the USSR, but many had been found abandoned in the Russian Theatre, not knocked out, but immobilised due to engine and other mechanical failures, arising from the unforeseen severity of conditions when operating in difficult terrain and a testing climate. He considered that the 12-cylinder Maybach engine gave a better overall performance than any used in British tanks. This was despite his acknowledging that the materials and workmanship seen in British engines were better, especially in those engines produced by Rolls-Royce.

The Russians had an excellent tank in the T-34, with a 76.2mm gun that he called 'marvellous', one of the most effective then in existence. But when it was first introduced, the commander had been expected to operate the gun, as well as manage the tank as a fighting vehicle, navigate, maintain radio communication and so on. A larger turret had subsequently been introduced, to provide space for the inclusion of a gunner. The Russian heavy tank KV-2 had a 650hp engine, with a novel compressed-air starter, but this had been more troublesome than the German inertia starter, having to be pumped up by hand to 150 atm and being subject to seizure due to condensation in cold weather. Contrary to claims, he had observed that Russian tanks were no easier to start in hard winter conditions than the German ones.

Concerning a matter that was to arise later, Cleff asserted that much more attention was required to the drive train of tanks. In all British and American tanks, (such as the Lee and Grant in British terminology), the gearbox was difficult to manipulate. The

Variorex gearbox was intended to reduce the physical strain on the driver in gear-changing, but he had reported that it was proving too delicate for desert use. The rear drive in British tanks was awkward to repair, and although they often had better ground clearance, their suspension was not as good as that fitted to German tanks. There had been national preferences for these – British and Russian tanks had often used the Christie arrangement, with horizontal coil springs acting through bell-cranks to react to the vertical motion of the bogies, whilst German tanks had used leaf-springs. But at this time, the suspension of the Mk III and IV tanks was about to be changed to torsion-bar springing, with trailing arms carrying a stub axle, which Cleff thought would become the preferred method for the future. The most suitable bogie arrangement was the Christie wheel, with its better air cooling. A compromise had to be made over wheel sizes. Larger wheels were desirable for covering difficult terrain, but smaller ones provided more points on the ground where large forces could be transmitted. This was important for traction, for stability on soft and loose surfaces and when firing the gun. For the 'tyres', the German artificial elastomer Buna was more hard-wearing than natural rubber. Steering systems in British, American and German tanks were equally good.

Although much of what was said might seem to be generalities, there was still interest in how they were seen from a German point of view. Summarising his opinions of the British tanks that he had observed in action, Cleff rated the Cromwell as a 'very good all-round tank' and the Churchill 'good, but rather clumsy', but considered that the angles of the armour of the earlier cruiser tanks had been misconceived, and from some directions were likely to deflect shells towards, rather than away from other parts of the hull.

He said that riveting had been found to be unsatisfactory as a means of repair, as it was impossible to effect good joints when sheets had been distorted by battle damage. But the German welding equipment available in Africa was not capable of dealing with anything other than minor repairs, so that damaged tanks that could only be repaired with proper workshop facilities had to be abandoned. Repair was made more difficult by the heat generated by welding affecting the hardening of external plating and armour, which was heat-treated throughout its thickness in manufacture. British practice was to harden a surface layer only. Although initial penetration by projectiles was resisted better by the harder face of the British product, the through-hardened German armour was better overall

German armour contained no nickel (for them already a scarce strategic metal). Analysis of the materials of construction of captured tanks did not accurately reveal the composition and treatment. It had been found that the French had developed a material for armour that was thinner and lighter than their own, but they had been unable to reproduce it. He gave no details, beyond saying that it was believed to be costly and to require raw materials that were no longer accessible. Use of light alloys such as duralumin might be considered in the future.

Questioned about spaced armour, which had been noted on some German Mark III and IV tanks in the North African Theatre, Cleff said that this was still something of an experiment. It had been found that interposing sandbags between an inner steel layer and an outer one of armour plate offered greater overall resistance to penetration. Although suggesting an analogy of it being safer to drive into a tree than a lamp-post, Cleff would not say whether this meant that fibrous materials were best for the filling, or anything about other materials that were being considered.

Cleff was told that another PoW had spoken of a smoke-laying tank that could travel at 60kph (38mph), driven by an engine with a speed of 20,000rpm. He had not seen this tank, but claimed to have heard of it, and he assumed that it was unarmed, so as to lay protective smoke screens quickly under covering fire. He considered that there would be a trend to smaller, lighter engines, with high rpm, probably simpler (eg two-stroke types), supercharged and using aviation fuel. There were similar trends in submarine propulsion. He had driven in a car that had an 800cc three-cylinder two-stroke engine, having great power and economy. He gave the impression that a radius of action for tanks as much as 250km (160 miles) might already have been realised in trials.

Supplying fuel and lubricants was a continual problem in tank operations. Cleff considered that oil usage would be high in British tanks, particularly for desert conditions, due to inadequate filtration. They had no counterpart to the German multi-plate filter, where the element was continually being squeezed clear of impurities by connection to one of the driver's control pedals. He was confident that Germany could supply all its needs for fuel, oil and lubricants by synthetic means from a feedstock derived from brown coal (lignite). He knew of the plant of STW (South German Fuel Works) at Breux, which drew its supply from coal mined in the district.

Military Intelligence was especially eager to learn about additions to the German arsenal that had not yet appeared in the Western Desert Theatre. Little had been known about the Mk V tank, but Cleff reported that in appearance it was the same as the Mk III. It was fitted with an armoured tower that was continued through the interior of the hull and supported on the floor. The commander and gun-layer sat within the tower, protected by its extra shielding. The ammunition for the 75mm gun was kept there, and it had an automatic loading device that rotated with the turret and dispensed with the need for a loader. He referred to this arrangement also in connection with a new tank gun of 88mm bore. It was said to be based on a mobile one of 75mm used by parachute troops, and to have a much reduced recoil. This too was to have automatic loading.

But he would not clarify seemingly incompatible statements that the cartridges for the ammunition were somehow loaded separately from the shells. A new shape of cartridge, though with the same quantity of propellant, apparently allowed ammunition to be stored more compactly, enabling more to be carried.

Information had been received from various sources about the Mark VI 'Tiger' tank, the latest addition to the German arsenal. It was known to have been deployed first in August 1942, but none had yet appeared in the Western Desert Theatre. Cleff thought that some had been despatched, but perhaps had been sunk in transit by the increasingly rigorous blockade of the Mediterranean coast maintained by the Allies. He was reluctant to give specific details about it, perhaps through knowing that interrogators from the locality had not seen one yet, beyond saying that it was a medium tank of less than 30 tons, long and low in build, to present a small head-on target, but in width it could 'go through where any previous German tanks could go'. He claimed that various models of the Mark VI had been tested in battle within the last four to five months. They had knocked out any tanks used by the Russians, including British and American ones that had been supplied to them in aid. At one point, while talking of the Mark VI tank, he had referred to the new 88mm gun, but when questioned would not confirm that it was intended for the Mark VI tank. Tested on the southern steppes, the Mk VI had successfully negotiated sand and sandstorm conditions much more trying than he had seen in Africa.

Specific questions had been sent to the Centre by the 8th Army, one of which was to discover German views about tank actions at night, which necessity had required the British to undertake, albeit with limited success. Cleff turned such questions aside smoothly, on the grounds that he was not required to have any knowledge of strategic matters.

1.3 Disposal

When the two summary reports concerning Cleff and interpretations of these were read at Military Intelligence (MI 10) in London, there was uncertainty about the reliability of some of his statements, but recognition that he was potentially an important source of useful information. This might include more experiences from his service in the Eastern Theatre; for example, he had already mentioned that the Russians had made extensive use of a mine with an outer casing of wood that contained no metal parts. German mine–detectors had not located a single mine of this type, and they had caused many casualties. Further, in one of his comments there had been an echo of Hitler's assurance to the German people that 'secret weapons' were being developed, that would be decisive in the war. This was a very active area for the intelligence services at that time, as they struggled to make sense of a multitude of scraps of information that reached them from many sources. Cleff claimed to know some details of what he called 'a new weapon more terrible and more powerful than any hitherto used', which made him 'shudder at the thought that it could ever be applied'. Beyond denying that this might involve chemical or biological agents, he asserted that he would never reveal what he knew about it. He thought however, that the weapon would not be deployed unless the British began to use poison gas.

The extent to which a sense of self-importance had reduced his caution remained uncertain, but it was decided that if he were transferred to Britain, further investigation might yet elicit more detail from him. A coded telegram was sent from MI 19 to the Commander-in-Chief, Middle East: 'Send P/W Hauptmann Herbert Cleff UK air earliest'. In the company of two British officers and one other PoW, he was duly flown from Cairo on 8 February 1943, in a No 511 Squadron RAF, Liberator Mk II bomber, AL561.

Chapter Two

Latimer House

2.1 A new situation

Cleff was taken to the main Combined Services Interrogation Centre CSDIC(UK), which was established at Latimer House. This was a requisitioned country house with grounds overlooking the Chess Valley, in Latimer, a village located east of Amersham in the Chilterns area of Buckinghamshire. Although in a rural setting, it had ready access to London via the railway from the nearby Chalfont & Latimer station. All three Services had contributed to the staff there, although their numbers were quite small. In 1943 the War Office (MI 19) and the Air Staff (AI(K)) each provided about a dozen Interrogation Officers at any time and the Admiralty (NID1) about eight. These were seconded from their respective Services and provided with their own supporting office personnel. The establishment was administered by the Army, which also supplied the group of monitors, who before enlisting had mostly been German-Jewish refugees. These manned the listening room, known as 'M-room', equipped to allow eavesdropping of conversations via the microphones that were hidden in all 'cells' and meeting-places. As the monitors were native German speakers, they could write down the gist of prisoners' conversations rapidly. If something particularly interesting was being said, and they could react in time, they could also record it for closer study (there were no electronic recording devices then, so these records were cut onto 12 inch diameter shellac discs, as in the first stage of making commercial records). Prisoners sent to Latimer were those considered likely to possess useful information, and another device used to tease this out was to put them on arrival with stool-pigeons, with whom they might exchange experiences. These were recruited from amongst willing German PoWs from all services, selected to be assigned appropriately according to the material being sought.

A more comprehensive picture of Cleff's life was built up gradually over the next few months, which might usefully be summarised at this point.

He was born on 28th September 1911, to a family which had become moderately prosperous through the development by his grandfather and father of the firm of Windmöller and Hölscher, of Lengerich in the Münster region of Westphalia. The company employed about 700 men, making machinery for the manufacture of paper products, particularly for packaging. It was substantial enough to have had agents for the UK and Ireland in London before the War, the firm of A Wantzen Ltd.

The young Cleff had shown keen interest in mechanical things, and an aptitude for mathematics and its applications. After completing the school-leaving certificate Abitur, he studied at the Technical High Schools at Darmstadt, Hanover and Berlin. In 1935 he received the Engineering Diploma (which in Germany entitled the holder to the prefix *Dipl Ing* to his name) with distinction in his chosen special subject of machine design with kinematics. This topic (the analysis of the motion of machine elements) was the subject of further studies with the guidance of Professor Föttinger of Berlin, with the intention of his submitting a *Dr Ing* thesis on the mechanism which he sketched, somewhat as shown in Fig 2. His choice of topic gives an indication of his way of thinking. The illustration is an example of a generic form of mechanism known in engineering as the 'four-bar chain'. It has many applications, in machines and equipment of all kinds, appearing in a variety of shapes, obtained by varying the relative lengths of the members. In use, one member is moved in a certain way, for example being driven around, if the lengths of the others allow it to rotate fully. The calculation of the connected movements of the other members was very laborious, when the available tools for that were only the slide-rule and tables of functions. It is probable that Cleff's doctoral thesis would have included ways of simplifying and speeding up the calculation of these motions. But it would have been in character if he had also addressed the practical difficulty facing the designer who wished to specify a mechanism to do a particular job. This involves the inverse process of obtaining the proportions of one that would provide a given output motion, as required by the machine of which it was to form a part. At that time, no systematic way had been devised for doing that.

Cleff's thesis had been due to be submitted in 1940, but was not completed, as with the approach of war, he was directed to gain industrial experience related to tank production, working successively at the Associated Steel plants at Bochum and Dortmund, at Rheinmetall Börsig at Düsseldorf, Alket, MIAG in Brunswick, Krupp in Magdeburg, and at the engine plants of Maybach, Daimler-Benz and MAN at Augsburg. This tour included every major plant involved in the manufacture of tanks in Germany.

From the end of 1937, there occurred an interlude, when Cleff was appointed to be one of what he called a 'triumvirate' (with two other engineers, who appeared to have been known to him for some time) to work at the Naval Research Station in Dresden. Here he was engaged in the development of burner design for a steam boiler plant, which provided opportunities for enlarging his knowledge in the areas of high-speed fluid flow and heat transfer. Then in 1939, he returned to involvement with tanks, accompanying the Panzer Corps in the German invasion of Poland and other actions, as related earlier. It now emerged that between the Polish, French and Russian campaigns, he had been called to Berlin for several consultations on tank design, and to the naval base at Kiel to attend to problems that had arisen with the boiler plant with which he had been concerned in Dresden.

It was clear to Military Intelligence that, through his education, training and experience, Cleff had acquired the combination of analytical skills, design capability and knowledge of manufacture that represents the highest competence of a professional engineer. There was good reason to believe that it would be of great value to learn about the German technical developments of which he knew from personal experience, but as with all sources there was a need to establish the reliability of his information. One of the reports of his interrogation in North Africa had noted his immaturity, the writer remarking that although aged 31 at the time of his capture, he 'looked 23 or 24'. He was now interviewed by Lieutenant Colonel H. W. Dicks, RAMC, the Psychiatric Specialist at Latimer, as seems to have been part of the usual routine there. Dicks produced the remarkably forthright report quoted in Fig 3. Here any sense of self-importance Cleff might have shown was elevated to the point of megalomania. Dicks was no lightweight, having been an intelligence officer in the First World War, and afterwards trained as a medical psychiatrist, becoming at some point a professor at Leeds University. But little evidence of such extreme delusionary behaviour on Cleff's part was on record elsewhere, and comments about him by others were never so lurid as this.

2.2 Army interrogation 2

Interrogation Officers in North Africa had managed to build up a good picture of his experiences, acquiring in the process some useful information in areas of interest to the Army. Even where this was not new, it could provide valuable confirmation when considered in relation to material obtained from other sources. This was supplemented by further comment on the Mk VI 'Tiger' tank during sessions at Latimer. He said that there were two versions. The first was a makeshift model, with a square hull, made to gain experience with the 88mm gun. Examples of this had been encountered in Tunisia, following the Allied landings in French North Africa in Operation 'Torch' of November 1942. (Although Cleff had been captured just before this operation, he would have been able to learn about this and other subsequent events from the British newspapers that were available to prisoners). The real Mk VI was larger and had sloping sides. It was equipped with a 105mm gun, of which there were two types, one being recoilless, although each needed its own version of turret. In the earlier model, traversing of the turret had been done electrically, but in the 'Tiger' this was hydraulic, the system also supplying drives for steering and gear changing. He claimed that the 'Tiger' could travel at an average speed of 55kph (34mph) 'across any country'.

Cleff also revealed that work had been done on the stabilisation of tank guns, to enable their aim to be kept on target when the tank was on the move. Tests had shown that the system would experience jolts with accelerations of up to 3g vertically and 2g laterally. The tank design would have to contend also with even bigger accelerations due to the forces arising from the recoil of the heavy guns now coming into service. He had personally taken part in firing tests with a tank having a special suspension, moving on a smooth concrete surface, but even there, satisfactory aiming results could not be obtained. He envisaged that the turret would have to be mounted in a 'cardanic' suspension (effectively in gimbals), a problem which, although difficult, he thought would not be insoluble. Further to the enquiries in Egypt about tank actions at night, he reported other tests with gyro-compass steering. The tank could be brought back onto its desired course when deviations from the compass reading had been noticed, but there would be lateral movements occurring in the meantime that could accumulate. The resulting departure from the required path could be substantial but would not be detected.

So far, he had been questioned only about tanks and ordnance, as might be expected, since these were matters on which he had direct experience through his specialist role in the Army, which he had now freely acknowledged. Although it was felt that he might have withheld other information that could be of use to the Allied cause, no further interrogations were conducted in areas of interest to the Army. No doubt the personal opinions that he had expressed, and the scraps of information revealed in passing, would take their place in the mass of material obtained from a multitude of other sources. These would continue to come in, and in time their real worth, if any, would emerge. That was in the nature of intelligence work.

However, Cleff's usefulness at Latimer was by no means at an end. From the monitoring of his conversations with two Luftwaffe prisoners, A(Am)43, a lieutenant bomber pilot and A(Am)90, a corporal, pilot of a 'Stuka' dive-bomber, it was learned unexpectedly that he also had knowledge of developments in aircraft and missiles, and that some of his naval work had been for submarine propulsion. These were all vital areas of concern at the time, and it is notable that the security classification of some of the documents relating to Cleff began to change from their previous rating of Secret to Most Secret, the highest level then in use.

Winston Churchill said later that the only thing that had really frightened him during World War Two was the effect of the German

U-boat blockade of the British Isles. This was now at its height, with Allied shipping being sunk at rates of up to half a million tons a month, threatening Britain's very ability to continue the war, due to interruption to the supply of military equipment, materials, foodstuffs and fuel from the US and other sources around the world. This grievous loss of merchant shipping, cargoes and personnel could not be endured for any length of time, and the intense struggle to contain, and eventually to reverse it, fully justified Churchill's term for it, The Battle of the Atlantic. It could scarcely be denied at the beginning of 1943 that the U-boat still had the upper hand. Any intelligence material mentioning submarines would capture attention immediately.

2.3 Naval interrogation

Cleff was now interviewed by Naval officers at the Centre from the Admiralty intelligence arm NID1. These sessions took place concurrently with others by officers from the corresponding RAF section, AI(K), but it will be convenient to review the outcome of the Navy ones first. This is partly because one of the officers assigned to interrogate him was to become a key figure in Cleff's future activities, and aspects of his own background are relevant here.

Donald Welbourn, Lieutenant(L) RNVR, had recently arrived in NID1, having been withdrawn from service in mine-sweeping operations, on the realisation that he had spent time in Germany before the war and was competent in the language. He had read engineering at Cambridge, and after a Graduate Apprenticeship at the English Electric Company's works at Stafford, had been retained as aide to the General Manager of the Works before being appointed Assistant to the Works Superintendent. By a coincidence, his work there had given him some acquaintance with tanks, the firm having been directed to join with the LMS railway works and Leyland

Motors to build the Covenanter 'cruiser' tank. It was a mark of the pressures in 1940 that it was necessary for the first hulls to be built at the same time as the new Tank Shop, in which they were to be constructed, was itself being erected. Although the Covenanter was low and sleek, with a quite modern appearance, it proved to be unreliable and difficult to maintain, so was never sent into action, being assigned to training and exercises for an expected role in home defence.

During these first years of the war, Welbourn's work placed him in a 'reserved occupation' (ie one in which he was considered to be making an essential contribution to the war effort, and so was exempted from military service), but in 1942 he resigned his post and volunteered for service with the Royal Navy. His highly-detailed memoirs include recollections of his first meetings with Cleff, with whom he was later to develop an enduring friendship.*

There were areas in which they were on common ground. Both came from moderately prosperous families, with fathers who were engineers in senior positions. Welbourn's Cambridge engineering course had been strongly analytical, and Cleff's inclinations had always been towards the use of mathematical formulation. This was the basis on which to build theoretical representations of the engineering systems under his consideration, and then to analyse their behaviour. The naval aspect of his experience had concerned the development of an advanced steam power system on which he had worked with two colleagues at the Naval Research Station in Dresden in the years 1937–1939. Welbourn reports that this diversion from his work on tanks had come about because he had been found the job there by Professor Karl Röder of Hanover, perhaps with a view to delaying his call-up into the Forces. Röder was being consulted on the development of turbines, about which he was a leading specialist.

---

* D B Welbourn – 'An Engineer in Peace and War', Vol I, 1916–1952, Lulu, 2008.

Although Cleff had been on Army service abroad thereafter, he had returned to Germany from time to time for consultations with navy people, having been last in Dresden in January 1942. He had seen his former colleagues in Berlin as recently as June. It was important to know these dates, as they would place his recollections correctly in the calendar of German technical developments built up from other sources.

Cleff would not reveal exactly where the naval research work took place, although he teased his interrogators by saying that the works were within a quarter of an hour's car drive of the Hotel Louisenhof in Weisser Hirsch, where he stayed when in Dresden (Welbourn found later that their work had been located on the premises of a privately-run company, Brückner Kanis KG, which made power turbines for ships, and for whom Röder had done consultancy work).

He seemed willing to describe the project in detail, and to employ the universal language of engineers – drawing – to clarify his account. This material provides an impression of his competence as an engineer, and might be weighed also in the assessment of the credibility of his claims to knowledge of other spheres of activity. And so the next paragraphs bring out some of the technical detail of the work on which he was engaged in Dresden.

The subject of the project was to produce a new type of steam-driven power plant, that could be adapted for a wide range of uses. Specific applications he mentioned were:

a) a 1,000hp unit of small size and low weight, intended for aircraft propulsion. This was built for testing, but up to the time of Cleff's joining the Army it had not been installed in an aircraft. Performance figures for this system are given in Fig 4

b) a 4,500hp unit, two of which were installed for trials in a *Schnellboot*, (S-boot, the high-speed torpedo boat known to the British as the E-boat, normally fitted with three 2,000hp Daimler engines),

c) units of 9,000hp or 15,000hp, installed in an experimental U-boat of 1,500 tons surface displacement.

In an aside, Cleff reported that trials had been made with steam-driven tanks, although not using the same system. Some had seen action on the Eastern Front, but had shown no advantages and the idea was not pursued.

The Dresden project had begun with the design of an oil fuel burner to deal with 5 tons of fuel per hour, but had then developed to include a combustion chamber and boiler to match, and finally a turbine to take maximum advantage of the boiler output. Fig 5 shows the novel swirl burner design, with the sketch made by Cleff at the top and an impression derived from this and drawn by a draughtsman to show more clearly how it worked. The air for combustion was blown at high velocity past the nozzle of the burner, passing first between guide vanes by which its flow could be adjusted to be as uniform as possible. In the nozzle, the high-speed flow of the fuel oil was made to swirl by helical guides, emerging as a spray to be further broken up and dispersed by impact with the air stream. It was arranged that only the smaller of the oil droplets produced could reach the combustion chamber, the larger ones, which would not burn completely, being removed from the outside of the spray by a rotating drum (the surrounding cylindrical assembly with V-shaped corrugations) which collected and returned the unused oil to the supply system. The boiler also had novel features, as shown by Fig 6, a drawing based on other sketches by Cleff. The boiler tubes were arranged in a ring of 24 elements, described by him as 'sections of the cake'. Any one of these could be isolated, removed from the boiler and replaced by a new one while the boiler was running at full power.

Fig 7 shows another sketch drawn by Cleff to illustrate the complete system. This is a closed arrangement, in which the steam is condensed after leaving the power turbine and returned to the boiler for re-use. Full attention is given in this arrangement to economy in service. Most of that is hidden in the complexity of an efficient steam–power cycle, but a straightforward illustration can be seen in the pre-processing of the air supply to the combustion chamber, shown on the left side of the sketch. Energy that would otherwise be lost in the heat carried away by the exhaust gases at the end of the process is recovered and returned to the air entering the system at the beginning. A turbo-pump driven by the exhaust stream raises the pressure of the air so that it can be blown into the burner section at the required high velocity, and its temperature is raised further by extracting remaining heat from the exhaust after it leaves the turbo-pump. This ensures the maximum practical re-use of the remainder of the heat energy released in combustion after it has done its job in the power turbine. Cleff claimed that the final experimental units of this type had burnt up to 15 tons of fuel oil per hour per burner, with a maximum overall efficiency of 29 per cent. Although this might seem modest, it was high in relation to contemporary practice.

Other technical developments were claimed in relation to this plant, including the use of steam speeds in the turbines up to 1,200m/s, with the alloys used for turbine blades having a composition of up to 90 per cent beryllium. There had been no engineering use of this element in Britain up to that time, so that its extreme toxicity was then unknown, and this claim seems to have passed without comment. But in an appraisal of the system as a whole by Lieutenan Commander(E) Stoddert RN, he concluded that it showed 'the utmost technical daring and originality … pushing steam and gas flow high-velocity technique to the ultimate limit of the possibilities of modern engineering and metallurgical science'. The efficiency and power/weight ratio were unusually high, but not irreconcilable with high pressure steam techniques and thermodynamic principles.

References by Cleff to the use of the power plant in submarines included claims that were disturbing. It had been fitted to an experimental 1,500 ton boat, built at the Germania Yard of Friedrich Krupp in Kiel at the beginning of 1939. By using a new type of fuel, the plant could be run when the boat was submerged, and the usual battery-electric propulsion system for this phase of U-boat operation could be omitted. This boat could dive to a maximum depth of about 600ft, and speeds claimed for it were 30 knots on the surface and 20 knots submerged. These figures were more than twice the typical performance of submarines at that time. The intelligence officer compiling the report even wondered if they had been taken down incorrectly, entering the query 'Should knots read K.P.H?' In kilometres per hour that would be the equivalent of 23 knots on the surface and 12 knots below, still ahead of the state of the art with the Allies. If U-boats could operate for long periods underwater and at speeds comparable with that of convoy escorts, they would be much harder to find and destroy

But these had not been the first references by prisoners to submarines being constructed with no provision for electric propulsion. Some were said to run submerged on their normal diesel engines, with the exhaust gases recirculated and re-activated by a supply of oxygen. A U-boat officer had spoken of a new class of small boats coming into service, of 500 tons displacement and a range of only 100 miles. They were turbine-driven and had no electric propulsion. Surface speed was 28 knots. Development had taken five years, and they had 'blown up many times'. Another had heard from a friend working at Kiel of 'experimental U-boats running on a new fuel, a sort of low explosive, looking like glycerine and producing no exhaust'. Again, there was no electric propulsion and the surface speed was 28 knots.

Cleff also spoke about the new fuel, since their boiler could run on it when the boat was submerged. Some of the claims he made for it were striking. It was usually in liquid form, looking like water, with a density 50 to 70 per cent of that in its various forms. He did not know its exact formulation, but it required no other substance or even oxygen for its combustion, as its general composition was $C_xH_{2x}O_{3x}$, so that the products would be just carbon dioxide CO_2 and steam H_2O. These would be compressed or absorbed and stored in the boat until it next surfaced. He understood that synthesis of the fuel molecule began with getting three benzene rings to join together in a 3-dimensional form. The oxygen components were then added, together with retarder groups to slow its reactivity. The fuel was safe to use, and would not burn in the usual sense – for instance it could not be ignited with a match. It had been used also in the reaction propulsion of aircraft. His most surprising claim was that the energy release in combustion was 90,000 kcal per kg. Today, this is an unusual unit, though it was readily understood at the time. To give scale to it, Cleff compared the energy with a value for petrol burning with air, which showed the new fuel to release about nine times as much as that. It was about 20 times a typical value for explosives, even though these too contained their own oxygen.

It might reasonably be said that in his interviews with interrogation officers from the Army and Navy, Cleff had, for the most part, referred to things that were already known, or were reasonable extrapolations from those. In general, he had not made startling revelations or claims that ran counter to their understanding of the state of knowledge on the Allied side. His reference to the secret new fuel and its applications was an exception to this. Something with an extraordinarily high energy release, that was being developed for use as a fuel with applications to the propulsion of surface vessels and submarines, was bound to require further investigation. But rather than by continued questioning by Navy interrogators, the topic was taken up as part of the investigation by RAF personnel, which was proceeding at the same time. This elicited further claims of applications of the new fuel, to the propulsion of aircraft and projectiles.

Chapter Three

Reaction Propulsion

3.1 RAF interrogation 1

Meetings with RAF interrogators, conducted in parallel with those with Navy personnel, were unexpectedly fruitful. The first report from these, AI(K)184A/1943, dated 11 April, bears the signature of Wing Commander S. D. (Denys) Felkin, who led the RAF team. It was made clear at the beginning that, unlike in his experiences with Army and Navy programmes, Cleff's own contribution to aircraft and projectile development had been very small; his only reference was to advising on problems in high-speed nozzle flow, drawing mainly on his Navy work. But this, together with some other aspects of tank operations where there were common interests, had taken him to meetings at Army and Air Ministry headquarters and to leading research establishments, including the flight test centre at Peenemünde on the shore of the Baltic, where he had seen testing in progress and been told about other activities.

As recorded in this first report, Cleff added that the new fuel had been one result of research by the firm of I G Farben into the production of petrol from coal. References to uranium and lithium in this connection were understood to indicate use of these elements in the synthesis of the product, perhaps as catalysts. Other particulars were as given earlier, but now he gave a lower value for the heat of combustion at 52,000 kcal per kg, but still about five times the figure he had given for petrol. Most of this energy, he said, came from the decomposition of its complicated molecular form. The familiar hydrocarbon fuels, composed only of carbon and hydrogen, required a supply of air to provide the oxygen needed for combustion. But the new fuel was said to be a compound that also contained oxygen, and moreover, in the correct proportions that would allow its complete combustion to carbon dioxide and steam. Something so self-contained is technically an explosive, and Cleff claimed that it had been considered for use as one, as well as in different applications as a fuel and a propellant.

He was asked about a propulsive device called the '*Do Gerät*', which had been mentioned by other PoWs. He could not throw any light on the origin of this term, but said it was a general one, referring not to any particular device, but to its means of propulsion, which was by the reaction to the discharge of a jet. The ordinary word *Düse* was used in this connection also, and could refer both to the jet and to the nozzle or other device from which it emerged. Figs 8a-8c show some sketches drawn by Cleff to illustrate the various types of reaction propulsion about which he spoke, and details of some particular components. There was much concern in British intelligence circles at this time about development in Germany of weapons for long-range bombardment, in respect of which scraps of information were being received from many sources. Sketch No 13 could have been relevant to this, as it shows a simplified rocket motor, using liquid propellant (which was found later to have been fully developed in the engine for the German A4 (V2) ballistic missile). Much time had been devoted to trying to understand the intelligence information, hindered by the assumption of some British experts that only solid propellants would be practical for such an application. Cleff now referred to rocket-propelled projectiles up to 100 tons in weight being in existence, if not ready for use. They would travel at 1,000m/s (ie three times the speed of sound). From his own calculations, he reckoned that one of these would need only 15 tons of the new propellant for a 500km range. Small ones that he had seen would fall within 25 metres of their target at 15km range. The recorder of this session inserted in the report that he considered these claims to be 'fantastic'.

The same term was also the one used by Cleff when he was told of stories from other PoWs about a long-range weapon that would kill anyone within two-thirds of a kilometre of its detonation. He ridiculed also a suggestion that Stalin had warned that the Russians would use poison gas if the Germans persisted with these projectile developments (although this also had an echo of a remark that he had made himself when interrogated in Cairo, to the opposite effect, that a terrifying German secret weapon would not be used unless Britain used poison gas first).

Other 'Do Gerät' devices described by Cleff took the form of what are called ramjets today. The principle is illustrated by his Sketch 1 amongst others, although his consistent representation of the intake as a converging duct throughout these sketches seems to imply that he did not realise that this would have made devices of this form quite impractical in use (this will be illustrated later, together with a conjecture as to a particular origin for the term 'Do Gerät'. If it referred to a specific device, a case could be made to reverse Cleff's opinion, and to regard the word Düse as the general term for propulsive devices of various kinds).

The ramjet is a propulsive device of the utmost simplicity, having no moving parts. The air entering the intake is caused by the varying shape of the duct to pass through the necessary thermodynamic cycle to produce the required high-velocity propulsive jet at the rear. Fuel, injected into the central combustion section and ignited in the air stream, provides the necessary energy input for the process.

Before the word ramjet came into use for devices of this kind, they were known in British circles as 'propulsive ducts'. Their potential had been reviewed by researchers at Farnborough in 1940, but they were thought to be unpromising, and were not pursued at that time. This was because the efficiency of this form of propulsion depends strongly on the forward speed, which is the cause of the pressure rise as the air enters and flows through the intake. It had been concluded that, to obtain a sufficient compression for practical use, the speed needs to be high, and to reach useful levels of efficiency, it would have to be flown at supersonic speed, for which there had been no applications at that time.

In the Latimer reports, propulsive ducts were called 'athodyds'. This was a contraction of 'aerothermodynamic duct', the term employed by the jet engine pioneer Frank Whittle. Welbourn claims that the abbreviation to athodyd was invented for convenience by himself and Felkin. As it is the regular term in the intelligence papers, athodyd will be used in references to them in what follows. From one origin or another, it came to be used generally for a time, although it has now fallen out of use, in favour of the word 'ramjet'.

Sketches 8 and 9 in Fig 8b show air being ducted around the outside of an athodyd, and driving a rotor immersed in the stream. In sketch 8, there are concentric ducts, with the rotor blades, driven as a turbine in the inner duct, extended to form compressor blades in the outer duct. The arrangement for the fuel nozzle for a combustion chamber, shown in these sketches with a surrounding shroud for collecting the larger droplets, is identical with that used in the naval boiler, seen earlier in Fig 5.

Cleff made several references to the application of reaction propulsion to aircraft. He was not impressed by the rocket motor for this purpose, which he appeared to consider at very best to be just a poor means of providing a brief period of extra thrust to assist take-off. The athodyd however had many possible uses. He described how it could be built-in to the structure of wings, and perhaps arranged as in Sketch 1 of Fig 8a, so that its thrust line could be varied by a few degrees as a means of control or maintaining trim. Several could be built into the blades of a propeller, as in Sketch 2, so as to provide the driving torque to turn it – he claimed to have designed nozzles and bearings for such an application (this was similar to the Turbine Airscrew that had been tested at Farnborough some years earlier, although there the compression was by centrifugal action rather than the ram effect due to rotation). Other sketches refer to various applications that he mentioned, although few of these seem to have had any practical use. Sketch 14 of Fig 8c was to illustrate a way of controlling the boundary layer flow on wings, by fitting a series of slots at the points where the flow normally broke away from the surface. The explanation of how this worked was not clear, but in any case the interrogator thought that Cleff had no direct knowledge of this subject, relying only on what he had heard or read about in technical literature.

As the RAF officer conducting the interrogation would hear Cleff's commentary as he drew the sketches of Fig 8, he would have more than the sketches themselves on which to base his judgment. But he made no comment on the little diagram on the left of Sketch 12. This appears to show a missile accompanied by two sets of geometrical axes, which could be recognised as part of a theoretical account of the stability of missiles in flight. The point that Cleff was making when sketching this is not recorded. If it arose only from something that he had read, there is nothing to indicate what the source might have been, or why he would have a reason to recall what would normally be of interest only to a very small group of specialists.

He went on to speak of applications of novel methods of propulsion to actual aircraft. He said that he had seen photographs of a flying-boat with a wing-span of 72m (236ft) to which these devices had been fitted. He also described an aircraft in which propellers were driven by opposed-piston IC engines (the 'boxster' type) at low forward speeds, up to the point at which athodyds in the propellers could take over the drive. When the aircraft had taken off, and a speed of 120kph (75mph) had been reached, the wing athodyds began to function sufficiently and the engines could be shut down. The propellers were then retracted hydraulically into the wings, with the blades in the horizontal position. The five athodyds in each wing provided up to 1,000hp each, and steering was effected by altering the distribution of fuel to the nozzles to vary the thrust. Either ordinary fuel or the new one described earlier could be used. Fig 9 shows two drawings prepared to accompany this interrogation report. These were attempts by staff at Latimer to illustrate what Cleff had described, since he had made no sketches in that part of his interview.

Cleff said that the cruising speed of this aircraft was about 1,300kph (810mph) and its maximum speed 1,800kph (1,120mph) at a height of 18,000m (59,000ft). On being questioned, he agreed that these were supersonic speeds, and by way of illustrating this performance, he added that it would allow an aircraft to fly from Berlin to New York in about three hours. The wing section for it, outlined, rather ineffectively, in Sketch 3 of Fig 8a, was said to be a compromise between that required for subsonic and for supersonic flight. The wings for this aircraft, with their athodyds already built in, were manufactured by Junkers and the fuselage by Messerschmitt.

There were references also to fighter-type aircraft, fitted with gas-turbine jet propulsion, which had been mentioned previously by other PoWs. According to Cleff, these attained a speed of 700kph (440mph). They were intended to intercept raiding bombers and had a very high rate of climb. They were easy to fly and manoeuvrable, but would often run out of fuel and have to land without power.

Projectiles might be propelled by rockets or athodyds or both. Sketch 16 in Fig 8c shows such a projectile with a rocket stage at the base. The athodyds would be ignited when the rocket part had burnt out. In Sketch 17 there is a ring of rockets outside the shell, allowing both types of propulsion to operate at the same time. Sketch 11 shows a cross-section to illustrate how a rocket could be mounted on a launching ramp, with support for its weight at A and guide rails at B1 and B2. Sketch 12 shows a projectile with four main athodyds for propulsion running right through the body, and four smaller ones facing sideways, which by applying lateral forces could alter the direction of flight, perhaps under control by radio signals.

3.2 A rapid response

The circulation of the first Air Intelligence report on Cleff's interrogation dated 25th April 1943 provoked a strong and immediate reaction. Amongst the recipients was Ben Lockspeiser, Director of Scientific Research at the Ministry of Aircraft Production (MAP). This massive organisation was responsible for coordinating the output of aircraft of all types as required for the three Services, from the wide range of plants throughout the UK where they were designed, developed and manufactured. Also within its remit were Government research centres such as the Royal Aircraft Establishment (RAE) at Farnborough in Hampshire, where firms could obtain advice and assistance from expert scientific and technical staff and have access to extensive capital testing facilities. Lockspeiser had oversight of the research programme here, and was now moved into prompt action, calling a meeting to discus the implications of the report, which took place on 4 May. This brought together a group of senior colleagues from the MAP HQ and other Departments, with people from RAE and the National Physical Laboratory (NPL) at Teddington, with leading university scientists who were also members of relevant Government advisory committees. Amongst the key personnel attending the meeting were:

Professor Sir Bennett Melvill Jones, Aeronautical Engineering, Cambridge
Professor G. I. (Geoffrey) Taylor, Cavendish Laboratory, Cambridge
Professor W. E. Garner, Chemistry Dept, Bristol
Wing Commander F. (Frank) Whittle, Power Jets
E. F. (Ernest) Relf, Aero Dept, NPL
H. (Hayne) Constant, Engine Dept RAE
R. (Ronald) Smelt, Aero Dept RAE

The discussion at this meeting concentrated on novel items in Cleff's revelations, particularly the possibilities of propulsion by athodyds, the supersonic aircraft and the new fuel. Although the use of athodyds for aircraft propulsion had been considered by the RAE earlier, it was soon agreed that a fresh review should be made of their potential, including their use in driving propellers and missile propulsion. Introducing the discussion on the high-speed aircraft, Lockspeiser spoke of it cruising at 800mph, with a maximum speed of 1,000mph at 59,000ft (although the figure given by Cleff of 1,800kph was actually over 1,100mph). The prisoner had acknowledged that these were supersonic speeds and had described some of the means taken to deal with the special problems of flight above the speed of sound. Frank Whittle told the meeting that he had gained the impression that this aircraft was actually in existence. Propeller power plant would be used to accelerate it to a speed at which the main propulsion from athodyds would take over, although he considered that the athodyd was a practical proposition for use only at speeds above about 500mph. Beyond this, its thrust would increase rapidly with increasing speed. As an example, at twice that speed, a duct of only 1 sq ft of cross-sectional area would provide 1,000hp at an altitude of 60,000ft. (This power figure was perhaps used for the example, because that was the familiar order of the power available from the piston engines of fighter aircraft at that time). It was agreed that trial calculations should be made on the potential performance of a hypothetical aircraft based on present designs of long-range bombers, but using athodyd propulsion and in supersonic flight.

On the new fuel, Professor Garner said that the low density quoted would indicate a hydrocarbon composition, but the reported heat of combustion was at least ten times higher than for known compounds. Whittle thought that the conditions in which the Germans were producing synthetic fuels might favour the discovery of new compounds that would not normally be formed at ordinary temperatures. It was agreed to pass the matter on for comment by a committee concerned with the high explosives industry, and to the Research Department at ICI, Billingham. It would emerge later that Lockspeiser had also sent enquiries to individual experts who might have a view on the claims for the new fuel.

3.3 RAF interrogation 2

The second report AI(K) 227A/1943, issued on 19 May, records amplification of Cleff's recollections during further interviews. He now claimed that at the beginning of 1942 he had witnessed the firing of a large projectile, without its warhead, from a railed launching-ramp 'at an Experimental Station somewhere in Germany'. It had been 5 to 6m in length and 2.5m in diameter, weighing 60 tons, with 15 tons of fuel, projected at launch by a rocket-propelled booster stage attached to its base, about 1m greater in diameter and 4m in length, and weighing 25 tons. For the purpose of this experiment, the ramp was located inside a steel-lined concrete pit, estimated to be 120m long, 75–80m deep and 50–60m wide, and raised by hydraulic gear to an elevation of 'a little over 30°'. From his position 25m away at the side, he first saw a small flame, then there was a huge billow of greyish-white smoke as the device shot into the air with a tremendous screaming noise. Its initial acceleration had been 8g (eight times the acceleration of a body falling under the effects of gravity). The rocket base had burned for 18–19 seconds and had fallen away after the device had travelled about 15km. Thereafter, the projectile continued under its own power 'out to sea' (presumed by the writer of the report to be the Baltic, although Cleff would not say exactly where), plunging into the water about 250km away. He thought that gyroscopic control of the path of the projectile was impractical, and hinted at a system of W/T (radio) control, constructed by the Askania company, that actuated four lateral nozzles at the base to change its orientation as required. The range was determined by varying the amount of fuel used.

Cleff added a good deal of circumstantial detail about this projectile, giving specific values of combustion temperatures and pressures, exhaust velocity, maximum speed and so on, although the compiler of the report considered that these had been conjectures on his part, rather than being given from actual knowledge. This was perhaps apparent also where these values raised obvious practical problems. For instance, having given estimates of combustion temperature 'probably of the order of 3,400–3,800°C', he recognised that that this was so high as to cause overheating, if not melting of the combustion chambers. But he reported that this was prevented by operating the nozzles alternately in two sets of three, to allow one set to cool by the passing air, whilst the other took over the propulsion. These details were reported just as they had been presented, usually without comment. Evaluation would be the task of the recipients given on the distribution list of the report.

He thought that the fuel for the rocket-propelled first stage had been a well-known chemical compound, probably in liquid form. This created a great deal of smoke as it burned, but the projectile itself was powered by the secret new fuel that he had described earlier. One of its combustion products was steam, although this was ejected at such a high temperature that no visible trail was produced. Cleff now reported that the lowest heat release from this fuel known to him was 35,000 kcal per kg, much lower than the two figures that he had given previously, but still more than three times the figure he had quoted for petrol. He had now become uncomfortable with the figures, acknowledging that they all sounded 'extremely improbable', but did not withdraw them.

The new fuel could also have had potential as an explosive. He described an experiment performed by I G Farben in the open, at their laboratories near Vienna. About 1cu cm of it had been placed in a hole bored in a 1m cube of lead. The hole had been sealed with sand and molten lead before the explosive was detonated. It had been intended that the energy released would be determined from measurements of the deformation of the block of lead, but instead of containing the explosion, the cube had burst, killing some of the spectators.

Asked about a 'rocket-bomb-torpedo' described by another PoW, Cleff said that this was a rocket-propelled bomb with wings, steered towards its target from its launching aircraft. He thought that the propellant was formed by two liquids mixing together, and that these produced large quantities of yellowish smoke.

He reported that almost the whole of the German aircraft industry had been experimenting with jet propulsion, beginning in 1938. His own knowledge dated from early 1942, when he had been shown a photograph of a Heinkel aircraft and was told about the high-speed Junkers/Messerschmitt machine that he had already described.

3.4 Other reports

A vital part of the assessment of intelligence information gathered from any source was comparison with that obtained from others. There was at least a reasonable expectation that confidence in the validity of an item of interest given in one account was strengthened if the same item had been mentioned elsewhere. Perhaps with this in mind, at the end of the report of this second stage of Cleff's interrogation a summary was given of information about jet and rocket-propelled aircraft that had been given by other prisoners at Latimer. This would have been a further possible contribution to building up the background of the state of knowledge of German developments at that time. .

A recently-captured PoW reported that when he was stationed at the Caen airfield in February, a senior officer of the Fighter Arm, General Adolf Galland, had made an inspection of the unit and while there had told the pilots about new aircraft with which they would be equipped next year. One was a Heinkel jet-propelled fighter that was capable of 800kph (500mph) and very manoeuvrable, and another was a rocket-propelled 'flying wing', which could climb to 10,000m (33,000ft) in two minutes. The latter jettisoned its wheels after take-off and landed on a cushioned skid on returning from combat.

Another prisoner reported that the jet-propelled aircraft was a version of the Messerschmitt 109 fighter, and had reached 1,000kph (620mph) in tests at Peenemünde. Others who had been at the Rechlin experimental station near Berlin thought that this was an aircraft called the *Schwalbe* (Swallow). Although using the same wings and tail as the Me 109, it was rocket-propelled and had a maximum endurance of nine minutes. Before its first powered flights, it had been tested at Augsburg as a glider, being towed to the required height by a (twin-engined) Me 110 fighter-bomber. It had been said that towing to operational height was being considered as a regular means of increasing its endurance as a fighter, the saving of fuel that would otherwise have been used in the climb thus raising it to as much as one hour.

Although reports such as these contained no allusion to the supersonic aircraft mentioned by Cleff, they would have been carefully considered. The references to the Me 109 was clearly a misunderstanding, as that aircraft was the general-purpose piston-engined fighter of the Luftwaffe, which had first flown in 1935. It had been in active service since 1937 when it had been involved in the Spanish Civil War, as part of the operations of the German Condor Legion, sent to aid the Nationalist insurgency there. Although it was developed progressively throughout the Second World War, by 1943 it had been superseded by the better performing Focke-Wulf Fw 190 (still piston-engined). It would not have been credible that a version of the Me 109 would have been chosen as a vehicle to introduce the new jet and rocket engines, as the performances claimed would have required aerodynamic forms very different from those of the propeller-driven era. There was indeed a Messerschmitt aircraft of very high speed, the Me 163, which on very little acquaintance had perhaps become confused with the Me 109. Prisoners might have anyway expected an involvement by Messerschmitt because of the widespread propaganda surrounding the capture of the world Absolute Speed Record by a German aircraft in April 1939. This had been described as an Me 109 for propaganda purposes, although it was actually a substantially modified airframe with a specially-prepared Daimler-Benz engine.

Reports such as these from prisoners would be welcome additions to the information coming in from agents and informers, and from photographic reconnaissance. Although these were often confused and contradictory, as in this case, enough material was to hand to allow a coherent picture of new German aircraft development to emerge. This vital work of interpretation was overseen by the Deputy Director of Intelligence (Scientific Intelligence) at the Air Ministry, Dr R. V. (Reginald) Jones, to whom there will be references later.

Chapter Four

The Enquiry Opens Out

4.1 Reprise

The third and final report on Cleff by the RAF interrogators was AI(K) 246B/1943, issued on 1 June. As will be related shortly, his attitude had undergone a change by this time. The reporter considered that it was now possible to distinguish more clearly between what he had actually seen, what he had been told – often by experts – and what was conjecture on his part.

He now said that at the beginning of 1942, when he had witnessed the firing of the large projectile that he had already described, he had been visiting a research station at Lettstäder Höhe in the Black Forest, located at 48°26'10" N, 8°15'40" E (no explanation was given for his being able to recall this position so precisely). He was there to consider the suitability of the new fuel for use in tank engines, but he had been smuggled in to see the launch of the projectile at a site nearby. Sketches that he drew to illustrate this are shown in Fig 10.

The launching ramp in its pit is shown in Sketch 1 (the projectile on it is not drawn to scale). Sketch 2 was to illustrate some point about the hydraulic gear used to elevate the ramp. The pit was built into the southern slope of a hill, was well camouflaged and capable of being covered by panels that extended out from the sides to meet in the middle and form a roof when it was not in use. The great width of the pit was to allow the ramp to be swivelled when the direction of fire was to be altered. The projectile he saw fired was aimed towards Lake Constance, the nearer shore of which was about 90km to the south (the previous reference to the sea might have been due to the German words for lake and sea being the same (*See*), although differing in gender). In conversations with engineers at the site he had learned that there were other stations for this kind of test – for example one south of Sagan in south-east Silesia and another south of Tarnow in Poland (about 70km east of Krakow).

Cleff now provided a drawing of the projectile as a whole (Sketch 3), with its rocket-propelled first stage attached. It was much as given previously, although he now thought that the diameter was nearer to 2.25m. The illustration of the devices used to propel the projectile itself (Sketch 4) clearly shows them to be liquid-fuelled rockets, suggesting that there had been confusion over nomenclature in the earlier reports. Except where rockets (*Rakete*) had been specifically mentioned, it seems likely that the term athodyds (which had been coined to refer to ramjet devices only) had been used more generally in translation, perhaps sometimes for the German word *Düsen*, which could be taken to mean any reaction propulsion devices. The cross-section shows the propellant contained at the rear, with a bay in the centre containing the pumps to convey it to the engines, together with the guidance system. The explosive charge occupies the whole of the front section. These details were almost certainly conjectural, like the indication that the shell of the projectile was 10cm thick. This totally unrealistic suggestion arose simply from Cleff having seen steel cylinders of that thickness and similar overall dimensions being made at the MAN works at Augsburg, which he assumed at the time to be for the bodies of projectiles. It was notable that the main missile was shown without fins. He now thought that the rockets used to propel the base unit used a solid propellant. However, he had not been able to tell the colour of their initial exhaust flame, as when he was asked about this he claimed for the first time that he was colour-blind.

Cleff's further remarks on jet-propelled aircraft indicated that his acquaintance with them must indeed have been purely incidental. His interest had been aroused when working at Dresden, where he learned that turbines being made there by Brückner Kanis were for a Heinkel aircraft being tested at Warnemünde (a station on the Baltic coast near Rostock). Then in 1942, he had been called to the German Air Ministry to discuss the transportation of tank engines to Russia by air, and whilst he was there an engineer had shown him photographs of three different types of jet aircraft. One was a Junkers/Messerschmitt project, with four engines in each wing, and 'double fuselages', inclined towards each other to join at the tail. It is not clear from the report whether this was related to the large supersonic aircraft mentioned by Cleff earlier, but this one did not require auxiliary engines since developments in jettisonable rocket packs enabled it to reach speeds at which the athodyd power plants became effective.

The second photograph was of a Heinkel interceptor fighter with four athodyds set in the wings, which he claimed actually to have seen at the Johannisthal airfield. It had a short fuselage, with a transparent nose, and was flown by the pilot from a prone position. He later met a pilot at München/Riem, who claimed to have flown this machine, which was capable of a maximum speed of 1,500kph (940mph), so was also supersonic. The third photograph was of an aircraft powered by eight athodyds, but he gave no further details of this.

Concerning the new fuel, he now said that it had 92 per cent of the density of water, with a translucent, yellowish appearance. He again asserted that its constituents were carbon, hydrogen and oxygen, but agreed that his reference to the use of uranium and lithium in its synthesis had been suppositions of his own. The laboratories at Leuna had been underground, 'partly on account of the danger of explosions', but he thought that they were no longer involved in manufacture of the fuel or experiments with it. The site had been suitable originally because its manufacture was an offshoot of the Fischer-Tropsch process for fuel synthesis (which presumably was being used there). On his earlier remarks about the explosive nature of the new fuel, he said that he had visited the I G Farben laboratory because of some concern about the control of 'unstable fuels'. He was unsure of its exact location, but thought that it was near the village of Edelsthal, about 50km east of Vienna. It employed 50/60 people, and a certain Dr Burckhardt was in charge.

4.2 Verification

The Army and Navy Interrogation Officers had been the first to bring their interviews with Cleff to an end. There seemed to have been little inclination to doubt at the time the account he gave of his own history and experiences. As to his claims about German technology, it is to be remembered that he could have known nothing of developments in Germany after November 1942, when he was captured, except for things that he might have learnt in conversation with other prisoners, which would themselves be of uncertain reliability. There would already have been further bits of information to be set alongside these references, from the numerous other sources being accessed by the intelligence services.

There had initially been questions about the extent of his knowledge, as for example on his claim that the weight of the Mark VI 'Tiger' tank was about 30 tons, when the first reports from the Eastern Theatre were already indicating that it was much heavier. However, his reference to several versions of this tank having been tested in Russia could have been a reflection of the fiasco in which

Porsche had put the design submitted by them into production before the first contract for the 'Tiger' had been issued. When that contract was awarded instead to Henschel, these earlier vehicles were adapted for heavy gun-carrying and other duties, and might well have appeared for test in the Eastern sector.

The timing factor meant that Cleff could not be aware of the shortcomings of the 'Tiger' tanks when they were used extensively in the Eastern Theatre. The effects of their higher failure rate due to their greater complexity was hugely magnified by their not having been designed, as the opposing Russian tanks were, with enough attention to ease of maintenance and repair in the field. A chronic tendency for German manufacturers to provide far too few replacement engines and other spares, both for tanks and aircraft, proved to be a crippling handicap. Amplified by the logistic difficulties of operating over such a vast Theatre, this became a significant factor in putting the German stance in the East onto the defensive after the end of 1942. Thus it was at least plausible that Cleff had been consulted about transporting tank engines by air. But although the 'Tiger' tank and its derivatives remained a continuing concern to the Allies throughout the rest of the war, Cleff's reports would inevitably recede into the background with the unfolding of events, such as the capture of an intact example in North Africa in the Spring of 1943, followed by its transfer to Britain for assessment.

As with the material from Cleff's interrogations on behalf of the War Office, that for the Admiralty was also largely taken at its face value, and would be overtaken in due course by more recently-acquired information. Their agreed conclusion had been that he 'would not wittingly give away information which he has reason to believe was not already in our possession', but that nevertheless what he did say would be useful in giving an indication of the trends in German scientific research. It was understood that the RAF investigator Felkin agreed with this view, although as previously reported, interviews about areas of aeronautical interest had continued subsequently. The most questioned of his claims arose in the three interrogations concerning aircraft and missile development, and the new fuel, which had been of keen interest to the Naval interrogators, had also featured there.

Welbourn had been very impressed with Cleff's understanding of engineering matters, and with his intellectual capacity generally. He thought he had 'run rings around' the psychiatrist Dicks when under examination by him (and perhaps a belated realisation of that had led to the intemperate use of language when the report of Fig 3 was being written). It had been noted several times, however, that in subjects where his knowledge was limited he was 'apt to draw on his imagination' where he could 'see the possible development of certain scientific discoveries'. Three areas in particular where the credibility of his observations seemed questionable were those relating to the secret new fuel, the long-range projectile and aircraft for high-speed flight. Welbourn felt that, given time, Cleff might become willing to be more helpful towards clearing up these concerns. He sought, and was given, authority to work more intensively with him towards this end. That was to have a far-reaching outcome.

4.3 Progess with Welbourn

From as early as the beginning of April 1943, Welbourn had been seeking additional views on the claims made by Cleff from experts outside the Centre. Concerning those about high-speed aircraft and their means of propulsion, he and Felkin went to consult Wing Commander Frank Whittle, who was known to be an acknowledged authority on these matters, and was also the liaison officer between the Air Ministry and the Ministry of Aircraft Production. They saw Whittle first in his office, established at Brownsover Hall, an old country house near Rugby, and then went on to visit the newly-completed Power Jets manufacture and test centre at Whetstone. Welbourn had been fascinated to learn for the first time about turbojet engines, and was also impressed by the personality of Whittle. He knew that they had been contemporaries at Cambridge before the war, but could not recall meeting him previously.

Whittle's long struggle to gain acceptance of his ideas for jet propulsion were at last bearing fruit. The first engine installed in an operating aircraft had taken to the air in 1941 in the experimental Gloster E.28/39 aircraft. Ordered just before the war began, this aircraft/engine combination far exceeded the requirements of its Specification, and was eventually to reach a level speed of nearly 500mph. But there had been difficulties in getting jet engines into series production until that had been taken over by Rolls-Royce. The Gloster Meteor, the first British jet aircraft to enter service with the RAF, had already been ordered and would make its first flights later in the year.

Whittle had been a tireless proponent of the jet engine, which he knew could open a new era in the evolution of flight. He showed that its propulsive efficiency would increase with increasing forward speed, unlike that of propellers, which would always experience a limiting speed at which there would be a sudden drop in efficiency. This occurred as the combined speeds of forward motion and rotation brought the movement of the blades through the air closer to the speed of sound, something that had been noted before the end of World War One. With an exceptionally sharp and inventive mind, and with a solid background in engineering theory and practice, Whittle was always open to new ideas and ways of thinking. Whilst still a Flight Lieutenant, he had been present at a meeting to discuss high-speed flight at the Royal Aeronautical Society in 1937. There was already evidence of the failure of established theory to predict the characteristics of air flow over aircraft wings and propeller blades as their speeds moved towards sonic velocity (760mph at sea level, falling to 660mph in the upper atmosphere). The accompanying steep rise in the resistance to motion (the drag) caused some to doubt the very feasibility of flight beyond this speed. But in the record of the meeting, Whittle is reported as having 'desired to register a protest' against this view; he advised that it would be 'most unfortunate if anybody went away with the impression that such speeds were out of the question'.

Whittle was keenly interested in what Cleff had said about aircraft propulsion, and in the sketches he made to elaborate his points. As well as having thought that the developments in high-speed flight that had been reported 'may well be genuine', Whittle said that the claims had caused him 'to revise some of his own ideas on these matters'. Welbourn thought that the main thing had been that Whittle 'had believed the stories, rather than thinking them crazy'. He expressed particular interest in what had been said about ramjets. As he kept referring to them as 'aerothermodynamic ducts', Felkin and Welbourn had coined the abbreviated term 'athodyds' for them in the car on the way back, and this had appeared later in the technical literature, 'remaining there until about 1950'. It was noted that this term was taken up at the meeting called at the MAP to discuss the first report on Cleff's material.

Whittle had taken a supportive position at the MAP meeting, and at some point he had visited Latimer to discuss the issue further. Unfortunately, Welbourn does not record whether any meeting directly between Whittle and Cleff had taken place. His recollections are overlaid with the outcome of a conversation that had arisen over dinner, about the naval information that had been revealed, and the high-speed U-boats in particular. Shortly afterwards, he had been called urgently to see Dr Roxbee Cox at MAP, and found that Whittle had sent a paper addressed to the Minister, showing how a submarine could be designed to do 20 knots submerged, frequently mentioning information provided by a Lieutenant Welbourn. Having now been apprised of the background, Roxbee Cox redrafted the paper, omitting his name, and it had been sent around various people at the Admiralty. Someone had taken it seriously enough to do the calculations that showed that Whittle's idea was impracticable. But Welbourn was amused to learn later of the comments of others, who had simply written it off as a fairy story from cloud-cuckoo land, 'the sort of thing to be expected from an RAF officer trying to tell the Navy how to do its job'.

Following up Cleff's claims about long-range projectiles and the secret new fuel, Welbourn also visited Dr R. V. Jones, Deputy Director of Intelligence (Scientific) at the Air Ministry. At this time, enough had been learnt from intelligence reports to expect that Britain would at some point come under attack from long-range projectiles, but the nature of these and their state of development were still very uncertain. Jones was charged with evaluating intelligence material from a scientific standpoint, and was arranging photographic reconnaissance of the Baltic coast around Peenemünde, where there had been strong evidence that devices of this kind were already being tested. Welbourn realised that the prospect of long-range bombardment was being taken very seriously, but at that date reports received about a long-range rocket had not even agreed on its probable size. Cleff's claims had been included in the intelligence material, by the circulation of reports on his assertions at the highest levels. For example, the distribution list for the report on the second RAF interrogation AI(K) 227A/1943 reads like a Who's Who of the principal decision-makers of the time, including Duncan Sandys, Churchill's son-in-law, who had been designated to coordinate an assessment of the reality of the threat from long-range rockets, for the War Cabinet Defence Committee. Others notified were Sir Henry Tizard, Scientific Advisor to the Air Staff, Lord Cherwell, Churchill's personal scientific advisor and the senior intelligence personnel of the Admiralty and Air Ministry, including Dr R. V. Jones (given as ADI(Sc)). But Welbourn does not record that anything had been said at his meeting with Jones about the likely veracity of Cleff's claims. When he heard later of the heavy loss of bombers when the RAF mounted a major raid on Peenemünde, he knew that it had been a significant event and could only hope that the attack had been worthwhile.

4.4 A turning point

The further interaction with Cleff that Welbourn had requested had also come into effect. He had developed a method of taking walks in the countryside around Latimer with prisoners who had given indications of becoming disillusioned about Nazism and might be willing to reveal information that could help to bring an end to the war. On these occasions he took the precaution of having a .32 calibre pistol in his trouser pocket, although at no time at the Centre was there any trouble with a prisoner trying to escape.

This process was used with Cleff, and in the time spent walking together, it was natural that they discussed aspects of their common profession of engineering. But, no doubt at Welbourn's prompting, they also discussed issues in European affairs, and philosophical matters such as the implications of Edith Cavell's assertion that 'patriotism is not enough'. As Cleff read and spoke English fluently, to stimulate further discussion Welbourn sought to lend him some appropriate books, although at first technical books were the only ones that he would read. From his arrival at Latimer he had made a point of using up much of his time in the solution of hypothetical machine design problems, into which he could become fully absorbed, and perhaps with a view to limiting opportunities for him to be influenced. A copy of Edward Titchmarsh's *'The Theory of Functions'*, which was relevant to that work, was readily accepted, and Cleff was seen to read it avidly. But it was noted also that he had taken the opportunity to read *The Times* thoroughly every day, so by perseverance he was persuaded to read a succession of books on modern European politics. In these were references to the statements of Martin Niemöller about the Hitler regime and to the treatment of Jews in Germany. What he knew of that had disgusted him at the time. He had known that his father too was alarmed at the rise of Nazism. To the displeasure of the local authorities, Dutch Jewish customers had been welcomed at their home, and ways had been found to shield workers in the factory who had Jewish connections. Welbourn reported subsequently that when at the Technical High School in Hanover, Cleff had refused to join the appropriate Nazi student organizations, and as a result was liable to be refused permission to sit an examination that had to be passed to continue his course. He was able to do so as a result of the support of Professor Karl Röder, who, although not a party member himself, seemed to have escaped sanction because of the double standards of the regime. Continuation of Röder's vital work on turbines for the Siemens company was evidently considered to be more important than his political sympathies (on meeting him after the war, Welbourn learnt that he had taken no payment for his Siemens work).

In his extensive experiences with the Army, Cleff had witnessed at first hand the ruthless means by which Hitler's plans to create a great German Empire were to be enforced. Welbourn recalls that he was 'shaken' by reports of the motivations of Nazism in the books of Hermann Rauschning that he was given to read, and wondered whether, in its drive to prevent the 'bolshevisation' of Europe, it had become more dangerous than Communism (it should be added here however that Rauschning's accounts of conversations with Hitler were largely discredited after his death). Cleff now began to discuss with Welbourn in a hypothetical way whether a duty might emerge to oppose the ruling ideology of a country, if it was seen to be harmful.

In this context they discussed also the status of the soldier's oath of allegiance, if the ideals it represented had been corrupted and provoked a crisis of conscience. He tried to address these matters with what Welbourn considered to be his 'high respect for reason, and a great love of truth, however unpalatable'.

In time, Cleff's personal position began to waver more distinctly. He resolved it eventually, though with an argument that was finely balanced. He could no longer bear the thought of a future Europe dominated by Hitler. The continuance of Nazi policies and methods would be disastrous also for Germany itself, so the war would have to be brought to an end swiftly, if there was to be any possibility of reconstruction of the nation along more acceptable lines. But he thought that Germany currently had the capability to win the war, so that one way of helping to end it would be by warning the Allies of the new weaponry that was being prepared there, so that measures might be developed to limit their intended effects. Yet however logical this might seem, he was deeply concerned that to play a part in it himself he would have to betray his country. Further, he had disturbing thoughts that knowledge of any action of his might get back to Germany, leading to reprisals being taken against his parents. He maintained consistently that any action of his would be solely in the interests of the future of Germany, although he worried that this might not be respected, and after the war had ended, those who had known him might regard him as a traitor.

It had been noted from the tone of the third RAF report that Cleff seemed to be more forthcoming than he had been previously. Now, on 26 May, nearly seven months after his capture, he confirmed that he was prepared to collaborate fully, and Welbourn considered that thereafter he did so wholeheartedly.

After the meeting at MAP in May, Lockspeiser had asked G. I. Taylor if he would see Cleff and try to get an understanding of his claims about the high-energy fuel. On a hot Whitsunday at the beginning of June, Welbourn and Felkin took him to Cambridge, where they had tea while lounging on the lawn of Taylor's house on the Huntingdon Road. Welbourn reports that there had been 'a charming and interesting discussion'. With their host were Dr H. Jones, a close associate of Taylor and John Lennard-Jones, Professor of Theoretical Chemistry, a considerable figure, who had made notable advances in the physics of the forces involved between atoms in the formation of chemical bonds. In a letter to Lockspeiser about this meeting, Taylor's account indicates that it might not have been quite as agreeable as reported by Welbourn. Asked what kind of burner would be used for the new fuel, Cleff had again sketched the one developed for the naval boiler system, shown in Fig 5. Taylor pointed out that this appeared to be a design for using a conventional fuel that required a supply of oxygen for combustion. Cleff had replied that it could be used with the new fuel by cutting off the air supply, but seemed uncertain when Taylor then wondered how the droplets would get into the combustion chamber if there was no air stream to carry them on. He then asked how fuel got from its storage vessel into the combustion chamber when it was used as a propellant in a projectile, but the vague replies he received about some form of pump had suggested that this had not previously been thought about.

Taylor had subsequently made some calculations of the heat output from various compounds, using his characteristic approach of estimation from first principles, on the basis of the energy required to assemble molecules and to dissociate them. He found that none came anywhere near even the lowest value of 35,000 kcal per kg that Cleff had reported. He concluded that no known circumstances could bring the heat output from any combination of carbon, hydrogen and oxygen atoms up to this value. In any case, if it was as high as this, the combustion temperature would be so great as immediately to melt a combustion chamber of any known material (in view of other activities in progress at the time, it is interesting that he considered but dismissed the possibility of some kind of 'atomic disintegration' being the cause of the high energy release).

Concerning the use of the fuel as an explosive, Taylor recognised the test, that Cleff had mentioned, to be 'the ordinary Travital test', a standard method of comparing the strength of explosives from the deformation produced when a specified quantity was exploded within a block of lead. Cleff had described cracks expanding outwards from the cavity that had contained the explosive, but Taylor noted that this was not the kind of failure that actually occurred in this test.

His conclusion from the meeting was that Cleff had probably heard about some new fuel, but that it could not have had the properties that he remembered. On the other hand, he thought that his description of the launch of a large projectile 'sounded genuine', although if it produced such a huge cloud of smoke, the propellant for the booster stage must have been burning very inefficiently.

Also on record are letters from other experts in reply to the questions about the new fuel sent out by Lockspeiser. One is from A. C. (Alfred) Egerton, Professor of Chemical Technology at Imperial College, an expert on processes in combustion, and sometime Secretary of the Royal Society. He dealt with the matter most thoroughly, going through the report of Cleff's interrogation practically line-by-line. To Lockspeiser, he returned an 8-page report, giving cogent reasons for concluding that the values given for the heat of combustion were not credible. Another letter was from Isaac Lubbock, an engineer from the Asiatic Petroleum Co, a joint subsidiary of the Shell and Royal Dutch oil companies prior to their merger, who was a specialist in combustion. He had provided the design of the fuel injection nozzles for Whittle's original jet engine, a key contribution that allowed a reasonable value to be obtained for the length of the combustion chambers, at a time when this seemed to be a serious obstacle to designing a practicable engine. Now, he was working on a rocket engine that would run on liquid fuels, something not previously attempted in British practice. Lubbock had been contacted about Cleff's report by William Cook, of the rocket propulsion section of the Ministry of Supply (MoS). Lubbock's conclusions are the same as those of the other experts, although he seemed to have been the only one to have found a compound with the $C_xH_{2x}O_{3x}$ composition claimed by Cleff, namely performic acid CH_2O_3. However, at that time this had been prepared only in an aqueous solution, and was not considered to be explosive. He also pointed out that hydrogen is often cited as having the greatest known heat of combustion per unit of its own weight, but this took no account of the much greater weight of the oxidiser, without which no combustion could take place. Comparisons by weight of different fuels should include the contribution of the oxidiser, if any was required.

Welbourn writes that in another excursion at about this time, he took Cleff to London, to the Maison Basque in Dover Street, to have a meeting over lunch with H. R. (Harry) Ricardo, the doyen of engine design, who amongst much else subsequently, had designed the engines for the first tanks in World War One. His extensive contributions to engine technology had covered many areas of practical design, together with penetrating investigations into the processes of combustion. The second edition of his monumental two-volume work *The Internal Combustion Engine* had appeared in 1931. In World War Two, his efforts were mainly applied to aero-engine development, and he was also a member of the War Cabinet Advisory Committee on Engineering. It was hoped that he too would be able to form a view on the question of the new fuel, but it seems that the conversation turned only on diesel engine design. Cleff had been flattered beyond measure to meet Ricardo, a figure who could surely not expect to learn anything new about diesel engines from him. At one point he had burst out "But all the German designs stem from your own book which we translated into German, and that has been our Bible ever since!"

4.5 The Lockspeiser Meetings

Following the meeting in May 1943, called by Lockspeiser to consider the first of the Latimer reports on Cleff, a second was held on 4 June, at which the contents of all three reports were reviewed. The first two had been circulated beforehand, but copies of the third, which had been issued only on the 1st of the month, were handed out at the meeting. Evidently, no time was being lost. Denys Felkin attended, to provide information on the background to the situation.

G. I. Taylor was again present, and reported his scepticism about claims for the new fuel. Surprisingly however, representatives of the MoS considered that the performance quoted for rocket-propelled projectiles was possible even with existing fuels. The significance of this in the context was that if confirmation of the reality of the projectiles was forthcoming in due course, that would not necessarily provide proof that a new fuel type had been used. On athodyds, it was concluded that the description of a large machine propelled by these probably referred to a jet-propelled project. The speed at which the athodyds began to work that had been given by Cleff was quite unrealistic. It was improbable that an aircraft could be accelerated to the speed at which they could operate effectively, even using assisted take-off rockets, owing to the very short duration of their operation. However, for the other aircraft that had been mentioned as reaching supersonic speed, athodyd propulsion might be appropriate, particularly if they could be somehow launched at a reasonable starting speed, say from another aircraft.

It was clear that the meeting largely discounted the reports of the new fuel. The aspect which exercised it more than any other was the several references that had been made to supersonic flight. Since the first meeting, Relf had written to Whittle to say that, after considering what little he could turn up about it, flight at supersonic speeds had seemed quite out of the question. But Whittle replied that it was known that the Germans and Italians had done work in this area that was much more advanced than any by the Allies. He felt that the evidence given by Cleff indicated strongly that discoveries had been made 'of such a nature that the aeroplane that had been described was a practical possibility'. His view would be highly influential.

It was decided that the group should form a standing committee to keep these matters under review. As will be seen later, the most lasting consequence of Cleff's capture was to emerge from the deliberations of this committee. Its driving force was the possibility that German science and technology had stolen a march on the Allies in this area, expressed in the conclusion of this second meeting: 'We in this country had not studied the problems of aircraft flight at supersonic speeds, but it was clear that there were many difficult problems, and if Germany had, in fact, solved them then that country was years ahead of Great Britain or the USA.'

Any concerns that might remain about the details of Cleff's testimony would be submerged by a fear that this was indeed the case.

Chapter Five

A Transformation

5.1 Further disquiet

Agonising about the opposing factors had put Cleff under great mental strain over some time leading up to his making the decision to collaborate, but that was not to end when he had made it. Rather it had been furthered, by other issues arising from communications with his family in Germany. These were received via the letters and parcels service for prisoners operated by the International Committee of the Red Cross under the provisions of the 3rd Geneva Convention Relative to the Treatment of Prisoners of War. Operating with remarkable effectiveness from its Central Prisoners of War Agency set up in Geneva, the ICRC oversaw the delivery of around 25 million letters over nearly six years of the war in Europe.

Under the provisions of the Convention, immediately upon capture, a prisoner was to be allowed to write a standard card to notify his next-of-kin of the fact of his capture, a statement on his health and an address for correspondence if known. Thereafter prisoners must be allowed to send and receive not less than two letters and four cards per month if they wished. These were usually written on standard forms, of which models were given in annexes to the Convention, and were necessarily brief. The text was to be limited to family matters only, so to check this they were subject to censoring by the authorities at both the despatching and receiving ends. This was allowed under the Convention, but any significant delay to delivery of mail was not.

Copies of some of Cleff's correspondence have been preserved in files at the National Archives, so in principle are readily accessible. However, having regard to their personal nature, references here are limited to matters that affect the unfolding of events and only to a level that illuminates that. Up to this point, his mail was addressed to Prisoner of War Camp 1, although no physical entity of this description existed, and it was forwarded to him at Latimer House. Most of his incoming letters were from his mother Elisabeth Cleff at the family home at Lengerich. Letters were also exchanged occasionally with his sister, living in Strassburg, in what during the German occupation was again known briefly as Alsasse. She was married to a Professor of Surgery, who was now serving with a parachute regiment, somewhere 'to the south'. At this time when Cleff's mind was already in turmoil, they had the sad duty of telling him of the death of his younger brother Wolfgang, who had been killed in action as a paratrooper on the Eastern Front on 7 February 1943. Welbourn recalls that Cleff had 'idolised' his brother, and in captivity had started to write for him a notebook on kinematics, a photostat copy of the first part of which he (Welbourn) later deposited in the library of the Engineering Department at Cambridge. The news of the loss of his brother was then followed quickly by that of his father Max, who had been ill for some time and died of natural causes on 20 February. He had been a strong influence on Cleff, and part of his inspiration towards engineering. Amongst other things, he had, by native ingenuity and common sense rather than formal training, doubled the output of a new item of production machinery at his factory. Subsequently, Cleff, to the satisfaction of both, had increased the output by a further doubling, by modifications based on the application of theoretical principles of machine design. Welbourn believed that a significant part of his motivation for working with his captors to bring the war to an end had been to continue his father's opposition to Nazism and what he considered to be its pernicious influence throughout German affairs. In contrast, his mother and sister were strong supporters of Hitler and his policies. He could not sympathise with that, so there was another source of disquiet at the centre of his family relations.

Other letters to Cleff were from a young woman Eli 'A', then working in Stuttgart (to preserve some anonymity, her surname is given here simply as 'A'. As other names arise, these will follow in the sequence 'B','C' etc). Eli believed that they had an 'understanding' as to their future relationship, and worried about the infrequency of his letters to her and the lack of appropriate warmth in his words. That he was receiving mail also from two other women, Ria 'B' and Gisella 'C', both of whom wrote in affectionate terms, would be unlikely to have calmed his state of mind at this time. These letters to Cleff addressed him as 'Peter', the name by which he was generally known at home. Welbourn called this his nickname, but there are indications that it was his second given name. From about this time, Welbourn must have been invited to use it also, as in his writings about him subsequently, he always referred to him as Peter Cleff.

5.2 Summer at Latimer

In the normal course of events, Cleff would have been moved from the Centre at Latimer House to a conventional prison camp, once it was concluded that no further information of any value would be forthcoming from him. As far as the Army and Navy interests were concerned, that point had soon been reached. But Welbourn thought that after his decision to collaborate, there could be areas in which his expertise in engineering could continue to be applied to the benefit of Britain. Under the terms of the Geneva Convention, however, there were strict limits on the conditions under which prisoners could be allowed to undertake anything that might be regarded as work.

Officers were permitted to work if they requested it, and there was a provision that a suitable occupation should be arranged if that was desirable for 'maintaining them in a good state of physical and mental health'. Normally, work by prisoners was confined to areas such as agriculture and forestry, but the Convention allowed occupation in others, as long as they had 'no military character or purpose'. Hours and other conditions should not be more onerous than those of the national civilian workers engaged in similar work, and prisoners should be paid, in accordance with provisions laid down in the Convention.

In that early summer of 1943, Welbourn made several approaches aimed at securing work for Cleff outside the confines of the Centre. Nothing significant developed from that, until on consulting his senior officer of the Naval Intelligence Department, it was suggested that he make enquiries from the professional associations for engineers in the area in which lay Cleff's expertise in mechanical design. The first approach seems to have been to the Institution of Production Engineers, where a possibility was considered that he might be employed at its own Research Department at Loughborough. This did not materialise, but Welbourn next approached Dr H. L. Guy, Secretary of the Institution of Mechanical Engineers. Welbourn had joined this body as a Graduate Member (so that Guy's first comment on meeting him was that an application to advance his grade of membership was long overdue). But Guy also had a suggestion about where Cleff's expertise could be used effectively.

Before becoming Secretary of the I Mech E, he had been
Chief Turbine Designer at Metropolitan Vickers, and had known
Claude Gibb (later Sir Claude) who before the war had held the
corresponding position at their principal rival company, Parsons
Marine Turbines. He was now Director of Weapons Production
at the Ministry of Supply. Welbourn went to discuss options with
Gibb and one of his Deputy Directors, Brigadier W. H. (Willie)
Blagden, at their Whitehall offices, and found them interested in
what was known about Cleff's capabilities. They were willing to see
him, and on doing so were impressed with his knowledge of tank
engineering, so that from the meeting there emerged a proposal that
he be employed there on possible improvements to the suspensions
for tanks and other track-laying vehicles.

Such an occupation would serve Cleff's purpose of helping to
bring the war to an end swiftly, but it would have been directly
contrary to the Geneva Convention, with its ban on work by a
PoW of any military character or purpose. The matter was however
not dismissed, instead being placed in the hands of a Major C. E.
Bellamy to explore whether the idea might be steered so as to come
into effect. For example, the possibility was considered that Cleff
might be released, and his status changed from that of a Prisoner-
of-War to a Resident Enemy Alien. This term had been established
under the Emergency Powers (Defence) Act immediately prior to
the war for a citizen of a foreign country who was resident at the
time when hostilities with that country had begun. It had caused
great difficulties for Germans and Austrians in Britain at the start of
the war, when they were all taken into custody, and procedures for
processing their cases were not yet in place. Temporary camps were
set up to accommodate them, including latterly some on the Isle
of Man. As ways were found to manage the situation, the majority
were released gradually and allowed to resume their lives and
occupations in the UK. Another possibility was that he be classified

as an Enemy Alien Refugee, used for those who had fled from the Nazi regime and sought asylum in Britain. But although these categories of persons existed, Cleff did not really belong in them, and so eventually an ad hoc arrangement was proposed, in which he would remain a PoW, but would be released from custody into the responsibility of the Military Intelligence branch MI 19. For Cleff to do the job envisaged for him, it would be required that he would have reasonable freedom of movement, and so it was established that such an arrangement would have to be approved by MI 5 from the security standpoint, and by the Home Office, which had the overall authority concerning the affairs of the civilian population. But it was anticipated that there would be difficulties in obtaining consent for such a radical scheme.

A detailed case was put together for submission to the Home Office, which drew heavily on a memorandum composed by Welbourn. In this he gave a condensed resumé of Cleff's time as a PoW, which will bear repetition at this point. He wrote that as Cleff was fluent in the English language he had talked with him practically every day since they had first met in March 1942. From close personal acquaintance, he saw that he was an extremely able engineer, in both practical and theoretical aspects of the art. It had been apparent from the beginning that he was almost entirely out of sympathy with the present regime in Germany, having shared with his father a revulsion for its treatment of the Jews and of objectors like Pastor Niemöller, and he had witnessed its brutality towards the Slavic peoples. Although he had been bound to set against this his soldier's oath to defend his country, he especially feared the threat to it posed by Russia, which his brother had died combating. As a prisoner, he had resisted moves to have him think about anything other than purely technical matters, but by his own inclination towards acquiring knowledge and much patient urging, he had begun to read about and discuss social and political issues.

He had come to recognise that Nazism meant eventual disaster for Germany and that it must be destroyed if there was to be any possibility of reconstructing the nation. In time, he had agreed to work with the British authorities to that end, but feared that all those with whom he came into contact would feel that this made him a traitor to his own country. On the other hand, with the possible future that he foresaw, it would perhaps be more traitorous not to act.

He was insistent that any help that he might give was for the future benefit of Germany, and he angrily rejected any thought that it might be for his own advantage. The strain of reaching the decision had been severe, affecting him both mentally and physically. Only by getting him into regular constructive work away from Latimer could this be overcome, and as he was capable of work that would potentially help to shorten the war two ends could be served.

However persuasive the case was thought to be, the wheels of bureaucracy turned only at their usual sluggish pace. Continuing to apply himself assiduously to technical exercises throughout the summer, Cleff began asking his mother, via his Red Cross mail, to have engineering books sent to him to assist with that, which she would be able to obtain from the VDI, the Association of German Engineers. The system seemed able to accommodate requests like this, and over time he received quite a number of works in that way, including standard texts such as:

Dubbel – *Handbook of Mechanical Engineering*, Vols 1 & 2
Baule – *Mathematics*, Vol 1
Bürklen – *A Mathematical Formulary*, and
Doehlmann – *Projective Geometry*, together with more specialised research papers for which he had asked, such as
Müller – *Thoughts on Theoretical Kinematics*, and
Flocke – *On the construction of curves by generating machines*

He was taken on another trip away from Latimer, this time to visit the Vauxhall Motors works at Luton, where the Churchill tank was being built. In 1941, the firm had been given just a year from the issue of its specification to have this heavy tank in production, and had met that requirement. This had included the provision of a new engine, which was designed around parts of a pair of existing 6-cylinder Bedford lorry engines arranged on either side of a new crankcase in a flat-12 configuration. With the haste required by the desperation of the times, there had inevitably been some remaining deficiencies, and the tank had moved quickly through several versions.

It was the Mark III that Cleff had seen in action in Egypt, and had rated it well among the British tanks serving there at the time. The visit to Vauxhall had aroused his interest, for on his return, he complained that data he had been given there were inconsistent. He argued that the three figures of 350hp engine-power, 38 tons weight and 30mph speed could not be reconciled. If the horsepower and weight figures were correct, he was of the opinion that the speed would be nearer to 30kph (19mph). There was concern that his willingness to collaborate, which had been so stressful to reach, would be jeopardised if he felt that insufficient trust could be established between him and the British authorities. He was quickly reassured that there had been no intention to deceive him. The discrepancy was indeed in the speed, which was about 19mph for the early Marks, just as he had predicted. And so his professional judgment was vindicated, at least in the area in which his direct experience had been most recent.

His mail from home was still unsettling. Eli had been hinting that they should become engaged, but he temporised, referring to the difference in their ages (he was 12 years her senior) and saying that he had not yet adjusted to the loss of his father and brother. His mother had sent him a photograph of his father, which he had not previously seen. It showed him sitting in his usual armchair, and this had affected Cleff deeply. He recognised that some of what he was experiencing was homesickness. Yet although his mother wished that he would write more often, he would say that he could not think of anything to put, as in a boy's letter home from school.

In one unexpected turn of events, his officer's trunk, which had not been forwarded to him up to the time of his capture, had been found somewhere in the Eastern sector and notification of that had been sent to Ria (probably it had contained a letter with her address). She had advised that it be sent to his home, and when it arrived there his mother wrote to say that she had received and unpacked it and nothing seemed to be missing. She asked if he wanted anything from it to be sent on. His request had been to have his Panzer uniform (presumably that would have been his best formal dress) and this was duly sent. In June 1943, replying to another letter from Eli, Cleff now said that 'her wish to be engaged was also his own', although this should not be made public until he had told his family about it directly. He appeared to be in no hurry to do that.

5.3 A new identity

It was not until August 1943 that the Home Office finally consented to the plan for Cleff's release and employment. There was a condition that no information about the matter was to be divulged within his lifetime and finally, according to Welbourn, that the docket authorising the action should be initialled by the Prime Minister, Winston Churchill.

Cleff was transferred from the keeping of DPW (the Department of Prisoners-of-War) and placed under the jurisdiction of Military Intelligence, MI 19. The formal acceptance of this was made in the letter of 26 August 1943, reproduced in Fig 11 (the rather quaint reference to receiving his 'body' was part of the terminology of the time – we might say 'person' today). In most respects, he would take on civilian status, and for that he was to assume a new identity, as Mr Peter Herbert, with the cover story shown in Fig 12. It is clear that this had been kept as close to real life as possible up to the beginning of the war in 1939. His date of birth was unaltered and the first names of his mother and father were retained, but they were given a fictitious address. Otherwise, the general location and evolution of his life were changed very little until it was necessary to omit any mention of his connection with the Army. He was then shown to have defected (escaped) when organising factory work in France, and to have made his way to Britain via Spain and Portugal.

Given the German propensity for meticulous record-keeping, this story would not have stood up to much examination by them, but it was intended only for any requirement that might arise in Britain. As far as the rest of the world was concerned, he was still a PoW. The ICRC were informed only that he was moving from 'Camp 1' to 'Camp 7', although both were merely mailboxes.

To help Cleff adjust to operating as a British civilian, on being released from Latimer House, he was first taken to live with Welbourn and his wife and their baby daughter. Their home at the time was not far away in the village of Ballinger, also in Buckinghamshire. The only formality involved seems to have been that his presence was to be notified to the Chief Constable of the County. He began to travel to and from London daily from Great Missenden station on the Metropolitan Line to Marylebone, thereafter making his way through the usual throng of commuters to his place of work at the requisitioned Hotel Victoria in Northumberland Avenue.

These early arrangements meant a good deal of travelling, so in September he was allowed to move into the more convenient location of a flat in Sussex Gardens W2, where the only condition was that he had to report his presence periodically to Paddington Police Station. Major Bellamy continued to have a general oversight of his affairs –

for example arranging for the payment of his rent and utility bills and reimbursement of expenses incidental to his work. He continued to receive the pay of £2 and 8 shillings a month appropriate for a PoW of his rank, but to this was now added a payment of £6 a week, tax free.

And so, less than a year after having been in the German Tank Army in Egypt, Cleff found himself living independently in London, with the assent of the British Prime Minister, and commuting daily to a paid job specially created for him, with an office in Whitehall next to that of the Director Armoured Fighting Vehicles.

Chapter Six

On the Ground and in the Air

6.1 Life in London

Cleff's work for the Ministry of Supply continued until beyond the end of the war, with occasional sharing of his effort with the Naval Engineering Department, although little of the detail is recorded. He was at first engaged in helping to sort out difficulties with the suspension of tanks developed by the Nuffield Mechanisation and Aero section of Morris Motors. These consisted of the cruiser tanks Crusader, Cavalier and Centaur. As elsewhere in British industry, there had been no previous history of this kind of work there, and under the pressures of the times the learning curve had to be very steep. Significant design faults were apparent in the Crusader, and its armament was no match for its German contemporaries, so it was already obsolete by 1943.

The Cavalier and Centaur were fitted with the 6-pounder quick-firing gun, and with greater attention paid to the requirements for efficient crew operations, proved to be more effective, although reliability was still a problem. When supplanted in due course by the Cromwell series, many of these earlier models were adapted successfully as mobile howitzers, bridge-layers and tank recovery tractors. The Morris tanks had large-diameter bogies, and would have provided material for Cleff's considerations of the relative merits of suspensions with these or with smaller bogies such as those used on the Churchill.

Welbourn continued to keep up his interest in Cleff in his new situation. As had been hoped, he had found his work to be absorbing, but it was noted that he continued to apply himself at a feverish pace. Although his life was now that of a civilian, there was little evidence that he had any interest in developing social relationships, either with his colleagues or others. The importance of outside interests had been pointed out before he started work, in a memorandum to Naval Intelligence from another branch of the Security Service. This referred to a previous case, in which a PoW had opted to return to prisoner status after working for some while. He had been influenced in this by what he read in the British press. Reports had convinced him that, after Germany had been defeated, the British people would insist on the imposition of very harsh sanctions on the country, as had happened after World War One. Although he still thought that it was right for Nazism to be crushed, he would not want to feel at the moment of his country's defeat and humiliation that he was partly responsible for her downfall and the retribution that she would suffer. The writer thought that there had been too little to occupy this man in his spare time, which had allowed him to brood over the strain on his conscience. It was rightly perceived that there was much here that might be relevant to Cleff's case also.

At this time, there was an unfortunate interruption to the mail between Cleff and his German correspondents, at least partly due to his revised mailing address not having been registered correctly with the appropriate directories at the British end. The bombing of German cities by the RAF was now building up towards its full scale, and perhaps also had some effect on the disruption of postal communications there. One result was that Cleff received several messages from Eli in short order, some of which had been sent months before, after his agreement to their becoming engaged. She had been overjoyed at this, and had made some moves such as buying rings for them and contacting his mother. She, however, had not yet received any news from Cleff about this. As a result, there were some recriminations and the progression that Eli had wished for was instead slowed down again.

In March 1943, the intelligence services had brought together two German Generals; von Thoma, who was captured in Egypt at around the same time as Cleff, and Crüwell, taken a few months earlier after being in a crashed aircraft. So far, they had been kept apart. When they were allowed to meet again, it was at a PoW centre for German Generals and senior staff officers, at Trent Park in Cockfosters, North London. Their conversation was monitored there, and it is reported that von Thoma had expressed surprise that, although they knew that they were in the London area, they had not heard any large explosions arising from what he called 'this rocket business'.

Hitler had promised the German people that new weapons were being developed that would wreak a terrible revenge for the bombing of their cities, and some detail of these had evidently become known to senior officers. Since long-range rockets had been mentioned by Cleff, perhaps he too wondered when they might arrive. It certainly continued to exercise the Government and intelligence staff. There had been fierce disagreements between experts as to the practicability of bombardment of targets in Britain, and on the likely effects if it did occur. Material from many sources, which would have included Cleff's testimony, had been brought to bear, but this was still too confusing to allow any definitive conclusions to be reached on the means of propulsion of such weapons. In turn, this affected estimates of the weight of warhead that they might carry and the potential scale of the damage they could cause. There were those, including Churchill's own scientific adviser Lord Cherwell, (formerly Professor F. A. (Frederick) Lindemann), who continued to disbelieve in their very existence.

Then, towards the end of 1943, evidence accumulated that a quite different threat might materialise first, one which had not been mentioned by Cleff. Along the great arc of the continental Channel coast facing England a new type of construction had appeared, eventually found at nearly a hundred sites, with concrete ramps aligned on London and some southern ports. There were various reasons why these would not be suitable for launching rockets; instead, they were more likely to be for another weapon that had been mentioned in some reports – a pilotless-aircraft or flying-bomb. In an account published after the war, *Evidence in Camera*, Chatto & Windus, London, 1957, Flight Officer Constance Babington Smith of the Central Interpretation Unit at Medmenham reported how she had spotted the first conclusive evidence for such a thing, on reconnaissance photographs taken from high altitudes over Peenemünde. When the large Army experimental establishment there had been heavily bombed in August, such damage was caused that its test work on rockets was transferred to other sites, including an inland range, far away at Blizna in Poland, but the airfield, a short distance to the west side of the peninsula, had not been included among the targets for the bombing attack. It was found that it was an outstation of the Air Force establishment at Rechlin near Berlin, the equivalent of the British centre at Boscombe Down near Salisbury, where new types of aircraft were tested before being accepted for entry into service.

Experimental aircraft had already been spotted at the airfield, including a flying-wing type, of a kind mentioned by PoWs at Latimer. Now, examples could be seen of a tiny aircraft of around 20ft span, which was designated 'Peenemünde 20' by the interpreters. Finally, one was seen resting on a construction similar to those that were appearing on the French coast. It was plainly a launching ramp for the little aircraft, facing along the coast of the Baltic for trials at full scale to be carried out. Babington Smith stated the position starkly: 'The most imminent cross-Channel threat was at last established beyond doubt. It was going to be a flying bomb.'

6.2 The Supersonics Committee

After its first meetings in May and June, the group of experts called by Lockspeiser to discuss the aeronautical aspects of Cleff's reports had been meeting monthly. It was never formally given a name, but as its papers were headed 'Problems of Supersonic Flight', it was soon referred to as the 'Supersonics Committee'. Its discussions were given the highest security classification of the time – Most Secret. Lockspeiser claimed later that his aim was to recruit 'the best brains in the country' for the Committee, and the membership included some of the most eminent and active scientific and engineering experts of the day in aeronautics. That these very busy people were prepared to give the time to meet monthly is an indication of the concern being felt that the Germans might have gained technical advantages of strategic importance in this area.

At its first meetings, the Committee had considered the claims made by Cleff about a new fuel, but after Taylor had spoken of his conclusions following his meeting with him, this was put aside as implausible. Its main consideration was the possibility of supersonic flight – that the Germans might have achieved it already – and the areas of work that would need to be explored to provide the data required for the design of aircraft to operate in that regime. As a basis for its considerations, it received from the RAE Engine Department an update of its 1940 review of propulsive ducts, (now being called athodyds, the term used in the Latimer reports). It was confirmed that they should be suitable for high-speed flight, but their propulsive efficiency would not become comparable with that of turbojet engines unless the forward speed was greater than around 500mph.

The Committee also received a paper each from the Aerodynamics Departments of RAE and NPL on the principal uncertainties in their areas. That supersonic flight was possible was not questioned, perhaps because aerodynamicists were well aware that shells fired from guns had been travelling faster than the speed of sound since the eighteenth century at least. What was necessary, was that in moving through the air, the shape of the aircraft would enable it to generate a sufficient upward force – ie lift – to support its weight, and that its means of propulsion would be able to provide a thrust force sufficient to equal the resistance of the air to its motion at that speed – ie drag. In both areas there was already some knowledge to go on, which enabled tentative performance estimates to be made.

Although it could be said that the principal characteristics of aerodynamics at supersonic speeds were known, there were many uncertainties that would have to be faced on the way there. The greatest difficulties were likely to arise in passing through a region from speeds below the speed of sound to speeds above it, say from about 80 per cent of that value (ie a Mach number of 0.8) to about 120 per cent of it (M = 1.2). Front-line fighter aircraft were already experiencing rapidly-varying forces and loss of control as they began to approach this region in powered dives. It was clear that, in addition to dealing with new conditions in supersonic flight, a whole new sphere of aerodynamics would have to be mastered to deal with this intermediate region. But the principal means hitherto used for research in aeronautics, by model testing in wind tunnels, was not available for that.

Attempts to design tunnels to operate in this region had so far failed, with no way found to circumvent an occurrence caused by a fundamental characteristic of the flow of air in the vicinity of the speed of sound. It had long been known how, by correctly shaping the walls of a duct, it was possible to accelerate air through that speed and beyond into the supersonic regime. But inserting anything into the flow near the region where the speed of sound occurred caused a shock wave to develop there. Instead of changing smoothly, the pressure of the air then changed abruptly over a very short distance. This was called 'choking' of the tunnel, and it prevented testing of models in that region, whether it was approached from a lower speed or from a higher one.

However, the Committee proposed to begin an initial programme of work to address its concerns. The first part would be to explore the characteristics of athodyds in free flight, with small model ducts propelled by the standard 3 inch solid-fuel rockets used in projectiles by British ground-attack aircraft. But calculations showed that these rockets would not be able to propel model aircraft of a reasonable size at sufficient speed for this. The Committee's attention turned to the potential for using heavy free-falling bodies with models attached for this purpose. These would be released from aircraft at high altitude, to see if they could, by accelerating under gravity, enter the desired speed range before reaching the ground.

As the Committee had no resources at its own disposal for this work, it was hoped that some of its official members, who held senior positions in their respective Ministries, would be able somehow to carry the main items of the programme within their own budget allocations. As the months passed, however, it was clear that the scope for this was very limited.

But now a change of direction began to seem possible, due largely to the enthusiasm of Frank Whittle. The first turbojet engines had flown successfully in various aircraft as test vehicles, although they had not yet progressed to full production for the service aircraft designed to accept them. Meanwhile, his Power Jets Limited had begun experimenting with a new layout – that in one form or another was to become the basis of most jet engines today, though was then entirely novel. This was done by using some of the energy of the exhaust jet of the basic engine to drive a turbo–compressor, rotating about the same axis, that would act on a second stream of air, in which more fuel could be burnt. The propulsive jet was then in the form of two concentric streams. These would enable a much greater thrust to be obtained overall, without a disproportionate increase in engine weight. Whittle suggested that this 'augmented' engine, which was already running at Power Jets in a preliminary form, might be the basis for moving directly to an experimental high–speed aeroplane. The design of that would not have to wait for the research and development of athodyd propulsion to be completed, and it would not be necessary to fit an auxiliary power plant to enable it to take off and accelerate to a speed at which the athodyd could take over. It would be able to take off, fly throughout its required speed range and land again in the normal way, under the power of this composite engine alone. This would, in effect, be behaving mostly as a turbojet engine in the lower speed ranges, and mostly as a ramjet at higher speeds, with thrust continuing to rise in the supersonic regime, as required.

It seems unlikely that Whittle would have failed to notice that Cleff had outlined something resembling the augmenter in Sketch 9 of Fig 8b, although there the secondary combustion stage had been turned around to fit the sketch onto the paper. He is not recorded as having mentioned this, but it would be expected to have increased his sense of urgency in the matter.

The Committee was taken with the prospect of being able to move in one step to an experimental aircraft for research into supersonic flight, powered in the manner suggested by Whittle. By its eighth meeting in November, it decided that there was a case for placing a contract on an aircraft firm to design and build one.

If Cleff's actions had unknowingly resulted in an ambitious forward step in this respect, his behaviour was disturbingly erratic at the personal level. Eli was now working for the railway in Stuttgart, training to become a station platform attendant. The work was very tiring, but her letters were full of enthusiasm over the implications of their engagement, for which she suggested that the notional date should be 1 June. Recently she had met one of Cleff's friends Heinz 'D', who had been home on leave, and he had told her about an arrangement of which he had heard, for marriage-by-proxy, which had been introduced for separated couples in their situation. She had contacted the Red Cross, which had confirmed that there was a procedure for this at her end. She asked if there was a similar one in Britain, and would he consider this? She was bewildered when in one letter he would make no reference to their future at all. He made no comment on the marriage-by-proxy idea, although at the end of the year he did go so far as to write that he 'longed for the time when he could call her his wife'. It is understandable that this vacillation would be very unsettling.

Very little is recorded about Cleff's work in 1944. But in his daily life, he could well have been aware of the growing signs that Allied forces were preparing to mount the invasion of the European mainland, as had long been promised. Ports and harbours along the South Coast were choked with shipping of all kinds, troop encampments were appearing near towns and villages throughout southern England, airfields were filled with transport aircraft and gliders, and road verges were becoming packed with military vehicles, equipment and stacks of stores of every description. Although strict security regulations were enforced, the imminence of what was to be the greatest seaborne military action of all time could scarcely remain unknown. The landing of Allied forces and their subsequent advance towards, and into German territory, would surely be fiercely contested and it would be natural if Cleff's thoughts about that would arouse further anxiety over the ambiguity of his position.

6.3 Miles Aircraft Limited

In support of the considerations of the Supersonics Committee, the MAP approached F. G. Miles, of Miles Aircraft Limited, to submit a proposal for the design of a research aircraft along the lines they were considering. This was a small firm located at Woodley, near Reading, conveniently near to Farnborough, and one that under a previous name of Phillips and Powis Ltd had a history of close involvement with RAE before the war. They adapted aircraft for experimental work at the Establishment and carried out flight research themselves under contract, on key topics such as high lift devices and boundary-layer control. Its main contribution to the war effort was to produce over 5,000 training aircraft of its own designs for the RAF, but from all its work it had a reputation for fertility of invention and innovation, and for rapid response to need. This was shown, for example, by its having designed, built and flown the prototype of its proposed M.20/1 fighter in just 65 days. It had also previously been approached by Whittle's company Power Jets with a view to a general collaboration, the first meeting between them having taken place in November 1942.

The specification put to Miles was remarkably brief. A small single-seat monoplane was envisaged, powered by Whittle's augmented jet engine, to be capable of a maximum level speed of 1,000mph at 36,000ft (at this altitude and above, the speed of sound becomes stabilised at its lowest value in the atmosphere, about 660mph). Little else was specified, except that it should be fitted with an all-moving horizontal tailplane. This would dispense with the usual elevator controls, which became ineffective through having to operate in flow over a fixed tailplane which became disturbed as speeds approached that of sound. By moving the tailplane as a whole, it was expected that effective control would be maintained when passing through the unexplored region between subsonic and supersonic flight.

Miles sized up the situation remarkably quickly and conceived an outline design, which was approved before the end of the year as the basis for a contract. And so, in a matter of months after Cleff had reported his recollections of German projects in high-speed aeronautics, a small British firm was to proceed with a research aircraft that would move in one step to flight at more than double the top speed of contemporary fighters, and for the first time beyond the speed of sound.

Chapter Seven

Turmoil on all Fronts

7.1 V-1

There had been no sign so far of a bombardment by the giant rockets of which Cleff had spoken. He might have had some concern about the prospect of that, as he was now living and working in the middle of the target area for which they were intended. But at this time, preparations were in hand to meet the more immediate threat of the flying bomb. This had not featured amongst his recollections, nor had any public warning about it been issued yet. It was to be the first of Hitler's 'reprisal weapons' (*Vergeltungswaffen 1* or V-1) to come into action, with plans for launching them in great numbers from sites along the length of the northern curve of the Channel coast. The principal target would be London, with some sent towards other targets within range, such as the ports of Southampton and Bristol.

However, accounts published after the war, such as that by David Irving, *The Mare's Nest*, William Kimber, London, 1964, show graphically how the opening of the campaigns with the V-weapons was repeatedly postponed. Allied bombing of the intended launching sites had caused the German Army to devise simpler equipment for catapult launch that could be concealed and assembled very shortly before use. New sites for these had been concentrated in the Pas de Calais region, north of the Seine, with a minimum of fixtures and improbable locations so that they were very difficult to spot. But then there were other delays, due to weaknesses in the management of the project, which were to have serious effects on all parts of the V-weapons work. A leading factor was failure to give sufficient attention in the design stages of the machines themselves to the requirements for large-scale manufacture. This caused a stream of modifications to be issued after production was supposed to have begun, resulting in numerous false starts and much scrapped work. Significant further delays were caused by vicious rivalry and manoeuvring for control of the projects between key individuals in the Army, the Air Force and the SS, causing much uncertainty through the issue of contradictory directives.

Information about these weapons, and even components from some that had crashed on test, were obtained by courageous individuals throughout the occupied countries and in Germany itself, sometimes at the cost of their lives in the attempt. Others, similarly at risk, transmitted that material via neutral countries to the intelligence services in Britain, and gradually an understanding of what the threats would entail was built up. The V-1 was the Fi 103 flying bomb, developed for the Air Force and initially put into production by the Fiesler aircraft company of Kassel. Code-named FZG 76 in service, it was a small expendable aircraft, of 5.4m (17.6ft) span, with a warhead of 0.85 tons of Amatol explosive. Most were launched from a short ramp by a catapult driven by steam from the decomposition of hydrogen peroxide, and in flight were powered by an engine that would be classified as an athodyd, as shown in outline in Fig 13. Rather than operating continuously, this engine had been designed to run in a series of rapid pulses, overcoming the tendency in athodyds flown at low speed for the combustion process to backfire through the intake. When pressure in the combustion chamber rose on ignition, a set of shutters closed the intake off, so that the exhaust gases could be ejected only through the exit at the rear of the duct to provide the propulsive thrust. Then as the pressure decayed, the shutters would open again, admitting a new charge of fresh air to serve the next pulse of combustion. The pulse repetition rate was 50 times per second, giving the bomb a characteristic sound, somewhat resembling a motorcycle. The engine, devised by the Argus motor works, ran on low-grade petrol, flying the aircraft at about 400mph at altitudes between 3,000 and 4,000ft over ranges up to 160 miles.

The accuracy with which the V-1 could be aimed was low, but London was a big target from such a short range. The direction of its flight was determined by an on-board magnetic compass, set at the launch site immediately before firing, which enabled some allowance for the effect of the wind to be made. The distance travelled through the air was then determined onboard by obtaining the equivalent of the number of turns made by a small propeller driven around by the airflow at the nose, which allowed for changes in the speed of the aircraft through the air during its flight. When calculated to be at the required distance from the launching point, it was put into a steep dive, for the warhead to explode on impact with the ground a few seconds later. As this system was self-contained, it could not be jammed. Apart from attacking the launching sites to prevent them being launched, the only defence against the V-1 was to intercept and bring down as many as possible in flight before they could reach the target.

Large-scale production of the V-1 eventually took place mainly at Volkswagen plants and in the underground Central Works near Nordhausen in the Harz mountains, worked by prisoners and slave labour. The result of numerous delays was that the first opportunity on which a salvo of these weapons could be fired at targets in Britain was not reached until 13 June 1944. But by then, D-Day had come a week before, when the Allied invasion to start the liberation of

Western Europe began with landings on the beaches of Normandy and the Cherbourg peninsula. However, it was not until October that ground forces were able to move into the region north of the Seine and overrun the launching sites, by which action the V-1 campaign was largely ended.

Over that period, about 2,400 bombs fell on London, although many more had been launched against it. The majority had failed due to malfunctions or had been brought down by the defences of anti-aircraft guns, fighter interceptions and cables trailing from balloons placed in their path. With experience, these actions steadily improved in effect until, on one day towards the end of the campaign, when 97 bombs crossed the Channel, only nine reached London.

Overall, about 6,200 civilians had been killed and about 18,000 injured, and tens of thousands of houses had been destroyed or seriously damaged, extending over a wide area. In the district of Penge in Bromley, south-east London, not one building escaped without damage. Some reduction in casualties and damage had been contrived by feeding false information to the German intelligence services, to the effect that many bombs had been overshooting the target. Accepting that information, the launch crews reset the timing to correct for it, with the result that they were then biased to fall short, in less densely-populated areas, although by no means in open country.

This was possible because all the German agents sent to operate in London had been quickly captured with their radio equipment and had been caused to send back convincing but misleading information. Despite these measures, it could be claimed that the V-1 had been a cost-effective weapon; its use did not involve putting aircraft or crews at risk, and estimates showed later that the cost of supplying one had been only the equivalent of £125 in 1945 money.

7.2 Life in London

Whatever he might have thought about events around him at this time, the file of Cleff's correspondence for 1944 is not lengthy, and makes dismal reading. In February, Eli writes of her concern that, after hearing nothing from him for two months following his declaration at the end of 1943, he made no reference to their engagement, as if it was not the most important thing in the world to her. She does not know how to respond to her parents' anxiety about her, and is now unsure whether she is justified in wearing his ring. Is there, she wonders, 'someone else'? Although it is horrid to speak so plainly of such matters, she feels no choice but to ask him to say clearly whether he does intend to marry her.

He had evidently conveyed his uncertain state of mind to his mother, for she writes that no–one would be more pleased than she, if he had found someone to share his life with, but only if he could make his commitment clear – she would not want to announce their engagement unless he did that. There is then another long delay, until August, when we learn that instead of confirming his intentions, he had asked Eli to release him from their engagement. This has to be inferred from her letters, as his own outgoing ones are not in the file, so the exact words by which he conveyed this message are not known. Her quiet dignity of expression in the face of his volatility is moving, and one is made painfully aware of yet another tragedy unfolding amongst the countless others in the world surrounding them.

Some concern must have been expressed to Welbourn about Cleff's state of mind, since in August he again interceded on his behalf, preparing a memorandum for Lt Col Rawlinson of MI 19, to summarise a discussion about it that had taken place between them. This covered five main areas:

- Cleff's present value should be high in his occupation at the Ministry of Supply, because of his known expertise and experience, and as this was being obtained very cheaply. Account should be taken also of original work that he was doing in his spare time, which was likely to be publishable. However, if he continued to overwork for much longer, his value would fall to nil.
- Cleff's future value to the country was potentially high, as he was a rare combination of a first-class practical engineer with a real mastery of higher mathematics. In the long run, he could probably best be used at a university or research establishment.
- Cleff's health had been the subject of a previous letter to Rawlinson from Welbourn's wife, Esther, who had been able to observe Cleff in their home for a time. She was a doctor, later to be a Fellow and Director of Studies in Medicine at New Hall, Oxford. Her view was to the effect that he might improve if a family could be found for him to live with, where his life could be more disciplined, although they knew from their own experience that this would require great patience and firmness.
- Cleff's attitude was that he now felt his work to be actually of little value, so that he was not pulling his full weight towards bringing the war to an end. This led to him chronically overworking, and as he seemed to have no outside interests a vicious circle was set up. His outlook had undergone a change, in that formerly he had wanted above all to return to his home and family business after the war, but what he had seen of the way of life in Britain had weakened the ties he felt with his homeland. He still believed that his duty would be to return to Germany, but only for long enough to put his family affairs in order and to make provision for his mother's future. He also had a fiancée there, although Welbourn thought that this tie was weak – evidently he was not then aware that Cleff had already purposed to break it off. Otherwise, he hoped that there was something he could do to help with the

rehabilitation of the country, although if the Russian influence was too strong then, that would not be possible and he would try to settle somewhere in Switzerland or England.

- Responsibility towards Cleff. No promises had been made to him about the future, but in view of his present unsettled state, this should be frankly discussed with him and if possible a loose plan decided upon. It was suggested that MI 19 should take this up with C. D. Gibb, with whom Welbourn had first arranged his present employment, because he might have greater knowledge of possible opportunities in industry, arising from Cleff's pre-war positions.

7.3 Another assessment

Welbourn's approach seemed to have led to an immediate action. On file is a report indicating that an opinion about Cleff's situation had been sought from a Dr Desmond Urwick, of Brompton Road SW3. He was then referred on to a consultant psychiatrist Henry Yellowlees (address not recorded), who replied on 9 September, after already having had two prolonged interviews with 'Mr Herbert'.

Yellowlees found that he was not suffering from any established nervous or mental disorder. His depression was 'a natural outcome of his circumstances and experiences acting on a person of his temperament and psychological make-up'. His physical symptoms (not specified) were secondary consequences of this. No real and permanent improvement to either would come unless his way of life was better regulated and his outlook became radically altered.

All aspects of his life had been disrupted, and he felt confident only in his scientific and mathematical work. Naturally, he was working this one outlet to death. He understood intellectually that there were other approaches to life and work, but he lacked the opportunity and the will to explore them.

It is notable that Yellowlees went on to reach conclusions that were essentially the same as those of Esther Welbourn. More than anything else, Cleff needed to have a few good friends of both sexes, ideally people of his own nationality, who were able to interact with him at his own intellectual level. Perhaps there were social clubs where suitable German-speakers could be found who would befriend him. But it would be 'a difficult and delicate task to get him to launch out' as required.

Yellowlees added that he did consulting and not treating, but 'this youth' (who in fact was then 33) had impressed him very favourably, and he would be glad to have a friendly chat with him occasionally. Being himself a keen chess-player, he wondered if perhaps Cleff might be induced to take up chess again, at which he used to be good, it seemed. He would ask Major Bellamy if something of the sort would be in order. This would surely have been beneficial, but there is, however, no evidence of it having taken place.

7.4 V-2

Around the time of the Yellowlees report, another disruption befell the people of London. On the evening of 8 September 1944, the first V-2 rocket arrived and exploded at Chiswick. Its supersonic speed gave no warning of its approach, the sound of which was heard after that of the explosion. Another landed that night near Epping. It had been mistakenly announced officially that day, that because of the Allied advance there was no longer any threat to Britain from V-weapons. But there was an area still under German occupation around the Hook of Holland, from which they could be launched and reach London within their range of about 200 miles.

Although much smaller than many had feared, this was seen to be a formidable weapon. As outlined in Fig 14, it was 14m (46ft) long, with diameter 1.65m (5.5ft) and was fitted with two pairs of fins at

1. Herbert Cleff in Panzer uniform (much copied, with loss of detail, but the only image located from before his capture). (National Archives)

Vorname — Surname	Name — First Name	Name des Vater — Father's Name
↓	↓	⌐ 189
HERBERT	CLEFF	→ Max Cleff

Date of birth / Geburtsdatum 28. IX. 1911   Place of birth / Geburtsort LENGERICH — WESTF.

Rank / Militär Grad Techn. K.V. Rat   Unit / Militär Einteilung

Army number / Erkennungs Nummer 1./Pz. Ers. Abt. 15 616   Last civilian residence / Letzter Ziviler Wohnort DRESDEN

Family's address / Adresse der Familie Max CLEFF LENGERICH — WESTF.

HANS — RICKMERSSTR. 45.

Coming from (Camp No, hospital No, etc.) / Ich komme von (Lager, Lazarett N° (u.s.w.)

Captured: / Ich bin Gefangener: unwounded* / nicht verwundet* — slightly wounded* / leichtverwundet* — severely wounded* / schwerverwundet* — ill * / Krank*

Am well* / Ich befinde mich wohl* — Am: recovered* / Ich bin geheilt* — convalescent * / In Heilung* — ill * / Krank*

Present address: / Meine gegenwärtige Adresse: Gefangennummer P.O.W. number 050747   Camp No / Lager No 308

Date / Datum 11. X. 42   Signature / Unterschrift Herbert Cleff

*=Cancel what does not apply / * = Nicht Passendes durchstreichen — No further details permitted / Weitere Angaben nicht erlaubt — See explanation on reverse side / Siehe Erklärung auf der Rückseite

Capture Card completed by Cleff, Egypt, October 1942. (ICRC, Geneva)

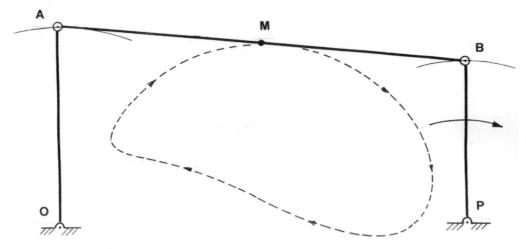

2. Typical 4-bar chain, the subject of Cleff's intended doctoral thesis. (B J Brinkworth)

The 3 members OA, AB and PB can rotate freely at their ends. The 4th member is part of the fixed frame of the machine between O and P. If PB is given a complete rotation about P, a representative point M on AB follows the path of the dotted line, showing how a simple mechanism can produce a complex motion.

"P/W M 164 gives the impression of having a one-track, furiously working brain mounted on a neglected over-grown child's body. From the age of four he has been obsessed with mechanics to the exclusion of almost every other interest. He has expressed himself completely content to sit alone indefinitely in his room in this camp doing complicated integral calculus, covering pages and pages with formulae and technical drawings, of incredible neatness.
In brief, this is a 'Franckenstein' personality, almost devoid of normal human feeling, a kind of calculating machine, whose only hold on life is mechanics and higher mathematics. He lives in a schoolboy world of phantasy à la H.G. Wells or Jules Verne, and while, no doubt, a very competent engineer, may quite well be weaving a good deal of inventive fancy into his constant preoccupation with these matters. It is a case of morbid genius very close to insanity by ordinary standards. Nothing in this note must be taken as justifying the conclusion that his more startling claims and theories need not be taken seriously. This is just the sort of man who invents destructive apparatus and takes a fiendish delight in the process, having no saner means of getting fun out of life."

3. Judgment of Cleff's personality by the RAMC Psychiatric Specialist at the Combined Services Detailed Interrogation Centre, Latimer House. (National Archives)
This view was not shared by others at the Centre.

Details of Aero Unit

Table of principal characteristics. The construction is generally similar to the unit described later except the turbine is single-cylinder, and the unit is designed for a short running life and extreme lightness.

a) Total weight of water in system 50 – 60 kg
b) Maximum steam pressure 1750 lbs/sq inch (120 atm)
c) Maximum steam temperature 1160°F (630°C)
d) Turbine exhaust pressure 30 lbs/sq inch (2 atm), zero wetness
e) Overall efficiency 31%
f) Turbine outer diameter 35 cm, overall length 145 cm
g) Turbine speed 36 000 – 50 000 rpm
h) Weight of complete unit 0.38 kg/HP
i) Maximum designed life 500 hours
j) Other figures in general as for 4 500 HP unit (Fig 7)

4. Characteristics of steam power plant for aircraft. (National Archives)

The reference to Fig 7 at J, is to another sketch of Cleff's not included here.

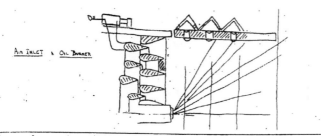

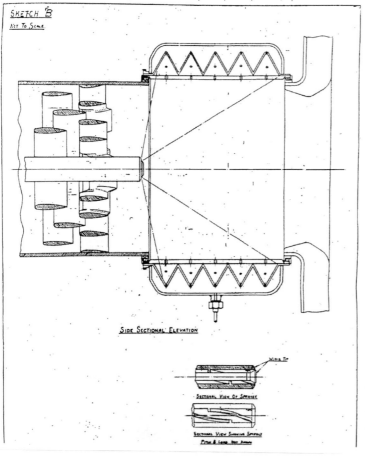

5. Arrangement of burner for experimental steam power plant, with sketch by Cleff at the top. (National Archives)

6. Arrangement of boiler for experimental steam power plant. (National Archives)

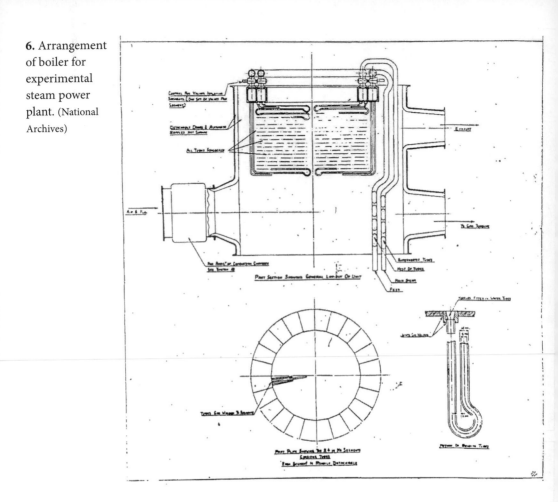

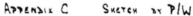

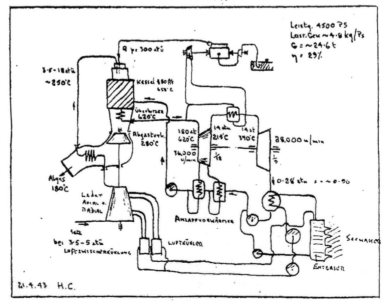

7. Sketch by Cleff of the connections for the steam power plant. (National Archives)

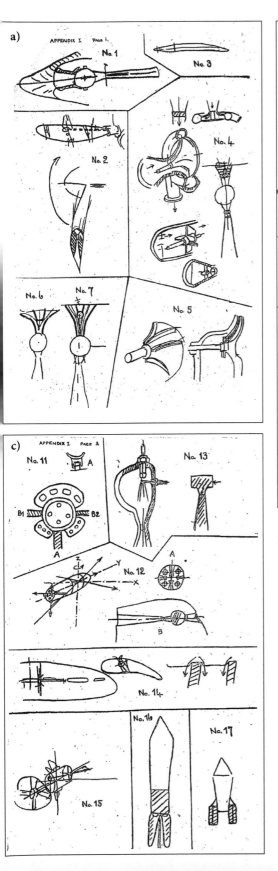

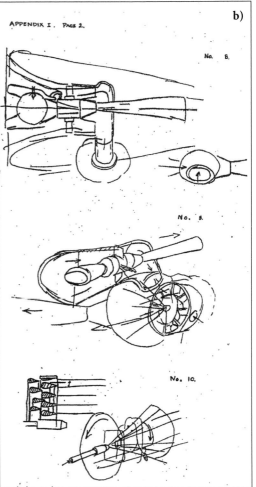

8. Sketches (a, b and c) by Cleff showing various applications of athodyds to aircraft and projectile propulsion. (National Archives)

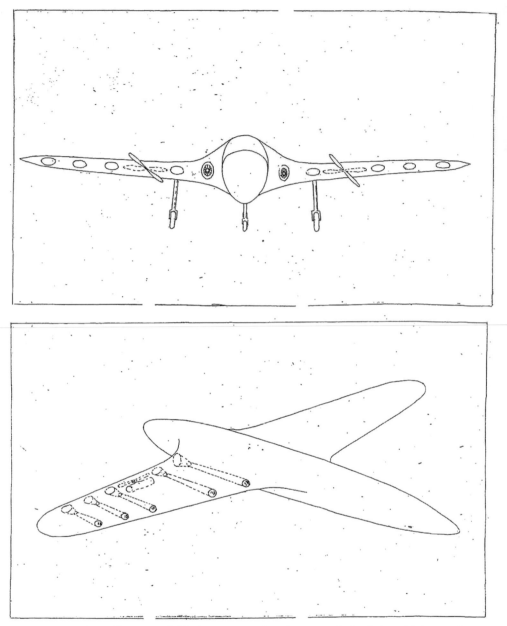

9. Drawings made to illustrate Cleff's description of application of athodyds to high-speed aircraft propulsion. (National Archives)
The absence of a tail is of no significance.

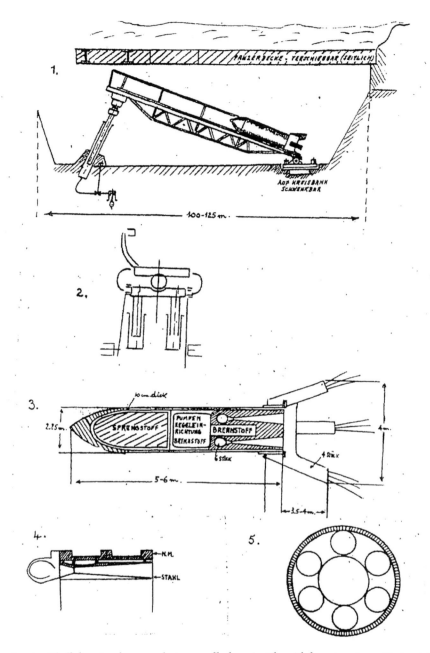

10. Sketches by Cleff showing large rocket-propelled projectile with booster stage. (National Archives)

11. Receipt for acceptance of responsibility for Cleff by MI 19. (National Archives)

LIFE STORY OF PETER HERBERT

Height 5' 11'
Weight 10 st. 8 lbs.

Born Hanover 28th September 1911

Father : Max Herbert
Mother's maiden name: Elizabeth Holler

His father died when he was quite young. His mother's address is Alleestrasse 129, Hanover

Schooling : Volkschule and Realgymnasium, Hanover

1931 Took Abitur

1931 Went to Berlin Technical High School and was then at Darmstadt Hanover Technical High Schools before returning to Berlin in

1935 where he took his Dipl. Ing.

Since that time he has worked at Vereinigte Stahlwerke, Dusseldorf and Hanover, Rheinmetall Börsig, Braybach, Daimler-Benz, Berlin and in

1936 was at Brückner Canis at Dresden.

Since that time he has been working in various war factories and in

1941 was sent to France to organise work for Germany in certain factories there. The middle of

1942 he managed to escape into Spain and thence, via Portugal, reached England about May of this year. Since May of this year we have had him under arrest, making investigations into his past, but we are now satisfied and have decided to release him to work in this country.

12. Cover story for Herbert Cleff as a civilian. (National Archives)

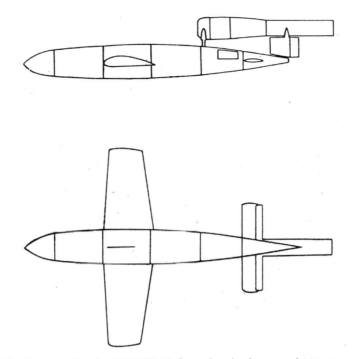

13. Drawing of the German Fieseler Fi FZG 76 flying bomb, designated V-1. (National Aerospace Library)

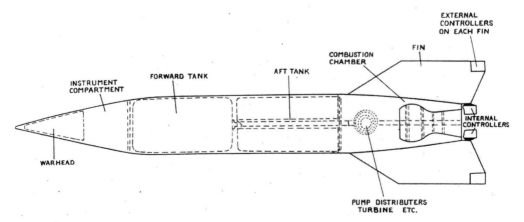

14. Drawing of the German A-4 ballistic missile, designated V-2. (National Aerospace Library)

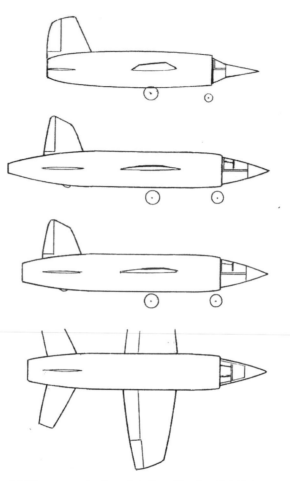

15. Evolution of the Miles M.52 supersonic aircraft to Specification E.24/43. (B.J. Brinkworth)
Top – Earliest known format. Second – First prototype, with jet engine only. Third – Second
prototype, with jet engine and thrust augmenter. Fourth – as third, plan view.

16. Model of the Miles M.52. (Farnborough Air Sciences Trust, FAST)

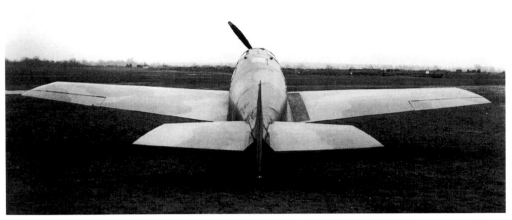

17. The 'Gillette Falcon', with thin, sharp-edged wing and tail surfaces and all-moving tailplane. (Miles Aircraft Collection)

18. Full scale mock-up of M.52, before skinning and attachment of wing and tailplane. (Miles Aircraft Collection)

19. 500mm diameter Sänger ramjet test-flown on a Dornier Do17Z aircraft, March 1942. (NATO Advisory Group for Aeronautical Research & Development, AGARD)

20. Captured German aircraft, in British markings for evaluation in flight at Farnborough, 1944/45. (National Aerospace Library)

Me262 with turboket propulsion.

Me163 with hydrogen peroxide rocket propulsion.

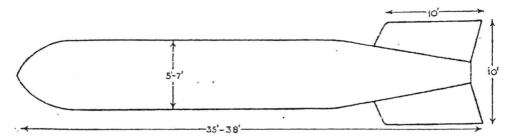

21. Sketch showing 'the limit of British knowledge' about the German long-range rocket in mid-1943, according to R. V. Jones. (R. V. Jones, 'Most Secret War', reproduced by permission of Dorling Kindersley Ltd)

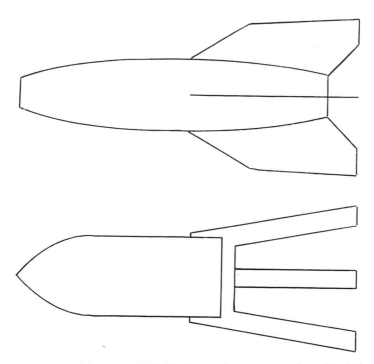

22. Outlines showing a possible origin of Cleff's ideas on long-range rockets. (*Top*) The A10 booster stage of the two-stage A10/A9 vehicle. (*Bottom*) Projectile shown in Cleff's sketch 3, Fig 10, redrawn in correct proportion, at twice scale of A10. (B. J. Brinkworth)

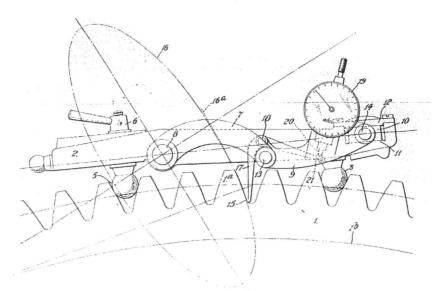

23. Cleff's measuring device for checking the accuracy of gear tooth forms. (Espacenet, via Intellectual Property Office)

24. Model of RT136, the first prototype of the Miles M.52, as planned at time of cancellation in 1946. (Photograph by B. J. Brinkworth)

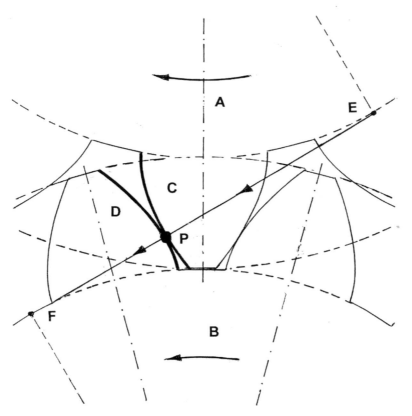

25. Construction of the involute curves that give the shape of gear teeth to engage correctly, showing the form to be reproduced by Cleff's gear-grinding machine. (B. J. Brinkworth)

Two gears A and B rotate together in the directions shown with A driving B through the pair of teeth C and D, which at this moment are in contact at P. A cord is imagined unwinding from a drum on A and being wound onto a drum on B so as to keep it taut. Any point on the cord then moves along the line from E to F. As the gears and drums rotate a point on the cord such as P traces out the curve on C shown by a heavy line. This curve is the involute that forms the correct profile for the contact surfaces on C. If the gears turn in the opposite direction, a point such as P moving from F to E traces out a corresponding involute on the other tooth D, also shown by a heavy line. The two curves marked heavily form the shapes required for the teeth to engage correctly throughout their motion.

26. Rare photograph of Peter Cleff, with *Haustochter* Eva Ruegg, on holiday with Welbourn family, Exmouth 1948. (D. B. Welbourn, 'An Engineer in Peace and War, Vol. 3, via Margaret Hardy)

the rear. Its weight at launch was 12.7 tons, including the fuel (a 3:1 mixture of ethyl alcohol and water) and oxidiser (liquid oxygen) with the warhead of about 1 ton of explosive. It was launched from a vertical position, being kept upright in the earliest stages of flight by carbon vanes controlling the deflection of the rocket exhaust until it was moving quickly enough for the fins and rudders to maintain stability and control. To give it the required range, its path was slowly turned towards the target and then continued to a maximum height of about 90km (56 miles) before completing its journey on a ballistic trajectory.

Efforts were made in its design to ensure that there would be no defence against the V-2. Although some used radio for the transmission of guidance signals from a ground station, that was vulnerable in principle to jamming. An on-board control system had been devised by the Askania company, (as mentioned by Cleff), and was used for the majority of the missiles fired in service. This maintained the direction of flight within the vertical plane joining the launch point and the target. Then from continually sensing the acceleration of the rocket, its velocity and position along its path could be determined by integration against time. The fuel supply to the engine was shut off when a point was reached from which the ballistic path followed thereafter would bring it to the target. This system is considered now to be an early version of what was to become inertial navigation.

Even in the terminal phase of its trajectory, when the denser air of the lower atmosphere had slowed it somewhat, the V-2 was still travelling much faster than the speed of sound. This had a minor connection with the supersonic aircraft project that Cleff had unwittingly set in motion. When Dennis Bancroft, the Miles Chief Aerodynamicist was leaving the National Physical Laboratory at Teddington, where he had been doing some tests in the supersonic wind-tunnel, a V2 fell nearby. Shaken by the curious inverted sequence of the explosion, the boom of the shock wave and the noise of the rocket rising up backwards into the sky, he asked what had caused them. "You should be telling me", said Dr Hilton the wind-tunnel chief, "for that's what your aircraft will sound like, when it flies past."

The V2 gave no warning of its approach, there was no realistic method by which it could be intercepted in flight, and opportunities for attacking it when it was being prepared for launching were very small. Fixed sites had been obviated by the introduction of the *Meillerwagen*, a 6-wheeled vehicle that could carry the missile to any suitable spot, raise it to the vertical, and when it had been fuelled-up, launch it over a base-plate resting on the ground and then move on. The bowsers carrying its fuel and the command vehicle were all nondescript and could not easily be identified.

As with the V-1, misleading information returned to the launch organisation by captured German agents again caused the controls to be adjusted, biasing the impact points eastwards towards less-populated country; but the dispersal was anyway wider than for the V-1, so that, out of about 1,200 rockets fired towards London, about 500 fell within the Metropolitan area. By the end of the campaign in March 1945, around 2,700 civilians had been killed there, with much attendant injury and destruction. But Londoners were not the only ones to suffer from V-2 attacks. Over 500 other rockets fell elsewhere in south-eastern Britain, and as the German forces retreated before the Allied advances, both V-1 and V-2 missiles were fired in quantity at other towns and cities in France and the Low Countries, with Antwerp, a vital port for landing Allied supplies, being the most bombarded city of all.

It had been expected when plans for a long-range rocket had first been detected that it would have a warhead of several tons capacity, and drastic measures were discussed for moving the seat of government out of London and evacuation of a large part of the civilian population from the target area. When it turned out that individually its potential for damage was not hugely greater than that of the V-1, there was puzzlement that so much scientific and engineering expertise, production capacity, materials and manpower had been allocated to it, particularly in what seemed like the most critical period of the war for Germany. Various estimates of the unit cost of producing the V-2 were made subsequently, but it seems that it might roughly have been about a hundred times that of a V-1.

7.5 An ending

Welbourn wrote later that when the flying bombs began arriving over London, colleagues had told him that Cleff joined the fire-watching teams on the roof, to observe the behaviour of these new weapons and to think about how they might be countered. He had not expected the V-1, but when the first rockets arrived, he would at once have been aware that they were so much less devastating than he had warned they would be during his interrogations. There could have been another addition to his state of anxiety if he thought that he might now be called upon to account for this discrepancy in some way.

His mail from Germany provided little relief. His mother wrote in August 1944 to tell him of having been informed by the Armed Forces ministry that he had been appointed in his absence as an advisor in the central organisation of the Reserve Army. From 1st April 1944, he was assigned to a career post in the equivalent of the War Office, with the substantive rank of Captain. 'Had he not always wished for that?', she asked. But at this time, further reminders of interests in his homeland seemed to be unwelcome, and were perhaps unsettling rather than reassuring. Then, in a letter from Eli she wrote that she had come to recognise that circumstances had changed for both of them; although in her opinion they should hold more firmly together because of that. She had lost so much, she said, that she did not know whether she could carry on 'without the certainty that someone is there to whom I belong'.

There is sad irony that the advice given to Cleff had been that the best way to deal with his depression would be for him to build relationships with people to whom he could become attached. But now he seemed to want to be disconnected entirely from those at his home. Despairing letters from his fiancée and his mother are the last in the file. At the end of the year, Eli writes that she has heard nothing from him since August, and is left in a state of 'confused disconsolateness'. In February 1945, his mother says that their correspondence seems to have been completely cut off, but sends him news of his sister's family and her own hopes that he is well, and remains of 'firm, unbroken courage and faith'. He had not told either of them that it was by his own choice that their correspondence had been ended.

Chapter Eight

War and Peace

8.1 The M.52

While Cleff's personal affairs followed their erratic course, he continued to work all hours at the Ministry of Supply, having in addition taken on some work on gearing for the Engineer-in-Chief's branch at the Admiralty. In the response to the effect of his reports on aeronautical developments in Germany, the team set up at Miles Aircraft Limited was also working at a fast pace. The contract to design an experimental supersonic aircraft had been issued against the Specification E.24/43, signifying the twenty-fourth project in the Experimental category authorised in 1943. At the factory, it was given the Miles type number M.52. It never had a name.

Like the business of the Supersonics Committee that had seen the need for it, the project was classified Most Secret, and knowledge of it at Miles was strictly confined to the small group of people directly involved in its creation. Apart from Frederick Miles (generally known as 'FG'), the Managing Director, and his brother George Miles (Technical Director), the leading contributors were L. C. ('Toby') Heal (manager of the team), D. S. (Dennis) Bancroft (Chief Aerodynamicist of the Company), H. S. Wilkinson (structures)

and D. L. (Don) Brown (systems). This gives a rough idea of the
principal division of expertise, but inevitably in such a small group
there would be much overlap and interchange amongst them, and
a few others became involved at times. The team, tiny compared
with the enormous forces assembled in later years, had to set about
designing an aircraft that would operate in three distinct regimes of
flight – subsonic, supersonic and the region intermediate between
these, known later as the transonic – in two of which there had been
no experience previously. But after an outline design prepared by
the firm had been reviewed by N. E. (Norbert) Rowe, Director of
Technical Development at the MAP, he had given the opinion that
the Ministry 'could safely entrust this project to them', and this
would prove to have been a sound decision, as far as it was allowed
to go.

There had been no systematic collection and review of information
that would be relevant to flight in the supersonic regime, and none in
the transonic. Despite this, Miles quickly sized-up the requirements
and arrived at a definitive layout for their machine, as shown in Fig
15. Their initial design, which had impressed Rowe, is shown at the
top, and the final form, in two versions, below.

The first aircraft of these two would fly with Whittle's W2/700
engine only, and was intended to explore the speed range from take-
off to as near to the speed of sound as could be reached. The second,
with the augmented form of the engine, was intended to pass through
the transonic region and onward to the specified maximum speed of
1,000mph, due to the greater thrust provided. The two versions of
the airframe differ only at the rear end, where the larger jet diameter
required for the augmented engine is apparent. A general view of
the shape of the M.52 can be gained from the model shown in Fig
16. It was a small aircraft, with a wing span of only 27ft (8.2m), less
than that of a Spitfire.

Although the layout was conventional, with fuselage, wings and tail unit in their customary arrangement, it was remarkably forward-looking and had many novel features. The fuselage, of only 5ft (1.5m) diameter, was the smallest that could contain the engine, the fuel tanks and all the electrical and hydraulic systems for control, retraction of the main wheels and much else. The cabin in the nose was just large enough to accommodate the pilot, almost lying back, with his legs raised above the level of his seat pan and astride a recess into which the nosewheel retracted. This cockpit was enclosed in a capsule, pressurised for high-altitude flying and cooled by heat exchange with evaporating ammonia when required to counter the kinetic heating expected to result from the compression of the surrounding air at high speed.

The capsule could be separated from the rest of the aircraft in an emergency, to descend stabilised by a drogue parachute down to a height at which the pilot could safely leave it and land with his own parachute. The air intake to the engine was in the form of an annular opening surrounding the capsule. On advice sought from Dr J. W. (James) Maccoll of the Armament Research Establishment at Sevenoaks, the overall shape of the fuselage and nose capsule was taken from that of the War Office's latest Standard Projectile, laid down in 1940. This basic shape had been established by a comprehensive series of controlled tests in the ARE's firing tunnels. These tests had determined the drag characteristics of bodies of this shape over the full range of speeds in which the M.52 was required to fly, and far beyond that.

The shape of the wings and tail unit was based on the first theory of wings in supersonic flight, published by the Swiss aerodynamicist Jakob Ackeret in the years between the wars. This showed that a wing could give a reasonable performance for flight in this regime only if it had sharp edges and a very thin cross-section. 'Thin' is here a relative term, representing the maximum depth of the wing expressed as a fraction of its width in the direction of the airflow. For the M.52, the team had conceived a sharp-edged wing having the high structural strength required for the task with a thickness ratio of only 7.5 per cent where it joined the fuselage, tapering to 4 per cent at the wing tip. The unusual cut-off shape of the wing and tail tips was an interpretation of an idea for reducing the drag, that had been put forward by the German aerodynamicist Adolf Busemann, presented at an international conference on high-speed flight in 1935.

It had been established as early as 1928 that the Ackeret theory gave a correct account of the lift characteristics of thin sharp-edged wings. This had been done by T. E. (Thomas) Stanton at the NPL (it is not generally realised that Stanton operated the first supersonic wind tunnel there in 1921). But it was necessary also to know the characteristics of wings of this kind in the critical stages of take-off and in flight at the low speeds that must follow that. To explore this, Miles modified one of their Falcon Six aircraft, fitted with wings and tailplane of the shape intended for the M.52, as shown in Fig 17.

At the works, this aircraft was known as the 'Gillette Falcon' after the well-known brand of razor-blades, because of the sharp edges of its wings and tail. Tests of this aircraft, flown by their own pilots and others at Farnborough, showed for the first time that an aircraft with thin sharp-edged wings could be safely taken off and operated at low speeds. In these tests, it was also the first aircraft to be flown with an all-flying tailplane, one that was moved as a whole to provide the only control in pitch (a feature employed widely on military aircraft today). This was to enable the pilot to maintain control during the passage through the transonic region, when large and rapid fluctuations of control force were expected as the flow adjusted to the change from subsonic to supersonic. The latest fighter aircraft of the day were already beginning to experience the effects of entering the early stages of transonic flow, when control by the usual elevators or tabs had been found to become ineffective in steep dives.

In another bold move, that would use technology for which there was still little experience, Miles proposed to use hydraulic power assistance for movement of the control surfaces on the M.52. By a system of its own design, this would provide the moments required to turn these surfaces, against air forces which were calculated to be much greater than had been encountered with any aircraft previously. Hydraulic jacks at the point of application would multiply the forces transmitted through the controls to levels that could not be reached by the pilot acting alone. The system would also hold them in position irreversibly. This would be important in also dealing with the fluctuating forces in the transonic region, and in avoiding the occurrence of 'flutter', a self-excited oscillation that had already been troublesome in subsonic flight.

From the autumn of 1944 and into early 1945, work on the M.52 moved on to the phase of detail design and preparation for the manufacture of the two prototypes. A wooden mock-up, a feature of all British aircraft design, was constructed to provide a visual sense of the airframe at full size in three dimensions, and to assist in ensuring that components could be fitted into their correct locations. This was built within an enclosure with strictly controlled access, but a few photographs of it survive, of which one is shown in Fig 18.

An event had occurred early in 1944 that could have been a major setback for the project. The Government had decided to create a National Gas Turbine Establishment along similar lines to the RAE and site it alongside the Farnborough airfield at Pyestock. This would be formed around Whittle's company Power Jets Limited, which would be nationalised, although for the time being that would remain on its site at Whetstone. Like the RAE, the new establishment would become a central research station, and would not be permitted to design and build any complete engines in its own right. This reflected the similar position after World War One, when the RAE, which in its original form as the

Royal Aircraft Factory had been doing a good job of designing and building aircraft, was stopped from doing so following complaints from private aircraft firms that this amounted to unfair state-supported competition. This new situation for gas turbine engines meant that the W2/700 would become the last complete engine to go into production at Power Jets. Eventually, the limitations of the new arrangement led to the resignation of Whittle and many of his senior staff, but the completion of the augmented engine for the M.52 seemed secure for the time being.

8.2 Priority

On 15 January 1945, Churchill circulated a directive to all Government Departments, that showed how the thoughts of the War Cabinet were already turning to the changing national priorities that would become necessary when the war came to an end. This required a review to be made of all research and development projects for the Services, with the objective that all those which were 'not likely to be used in operations on a considerable scale in the second half of 1946' should be cut. That would release research workers and draughtsmen, who were 'scanty', and were needed by industry in preparation for the change-over to peace-time production and for the development of civil air transport. The Minister for Aircraft Production, Stafford Cripps, asked for clarification in respect of a reference to 'the normal research and development essential to keep us ahead in types of Aircraft, Engines, etc'. With prescience, he went on to say that cuts in these areas would 'very gravely jeopardise our whole position in the air for many years to come, since once we lost our position we could never – in peace time – catch up again on other nations'. Churchill replied that it was not the intention that any such work should be slowed down or abandoned. Priority should be given to munitions likely to become available for use in the war against Japan, and other projects should be viewed 'with due regard to the broader needs of the country'.

When the priority list was returned for the MAP, the M.52 supersonic research aircraft was prominent at the top of the page.

8.3 German work

When Allied forces crossed into German territory early in 1945, there was keen interest among technical specialists of all kinds in finding out the actual state of development reached by the enemy in their particular fields. Answers had first begun to be obtained from the examination of captured equipment. Captain E. M. (Eric) Brown RN, who at that time was seconded to the Aero Flight at Farnborough, wrote of being given a mission to trace interesting types of aircraft, and if possible to fly or have them flown back to Britain for closer study. (see *Wings on my Sleeve*, by Eric 'Winkle' Brown, Weidenfeld & Nicolson, London 2006). These added to the total of different types of aircraft that he flew himself, which ultimately reached the record number of 487. With typical determination, he sometimes found himself ahead of the advancing forces, at one time having to accept the formal surrender of an airfield from its German Commandant, receiving the latter's ceremonial sword as the only Allied officer in the vicinity.

Much was learned by examining and flying these captured aircraft, but this needed to be backed by locating records of the theoretical foundations of the ideas involved in their design and the experimental data that provided the essential basis for implementation. Key German personnel were also eagerly sought for debriefing, and these activities became a race between teams from the four Allied powers, which continued after the end of hostilities, until it became practicable to divide Germany into four zones, each assigned to one of the allied nations for administrative purposes. This was an arrangement agreed in the planning for the immediate post-war period, in the belief that it would facilitate the management of the country until transition to a proper civil power could be organised.

Although it was known that as well as the V-1 and V-2 missiles, Germany had fielded several jet aircraft, a rocket-propelled fighter and various guided missiles, staff of the former MAP, now part of the Ministry of Supply, were stunned by what was returned by the exploratory teams. There were whole areas of aeronautical technology in which British work had proceeded less far, or had not been addressed at all. An obvious one was the use of rocket propulsion. In this an interest in potential military applications had begun in Germany in 1929. The possibilities of using liquid fuels had been appreciated from the beginning, whereas solid-fuel propulsion had been retained exclusively in British military rocketry throughout the war.

The guided missile was another innovation that had its origins before the war, although only Henschel's air-launched winged missiles – the free-falling 'Fritz-X' and the rocket-propelled Hs 293 – reached any significant operational use. Controlled by radio by an operator, keeping well out of range in the bomber aircraft from which they were launched, these weapons had some successes against shipping, mainly in the Mediterranean Theatre. From their seeming capacity to change course towards ships as they manoeuvred to escape, crews called these first guided weapons 'Chase-me-Charlies'. This was probably the missile recalled by Cleff when asked about a 'rocket- bomb-torpedo' that had been mentioned by another PoW. Henschel produced a version of the Hs 293 that was designed to enter the water at the end of its flight and to attack its target below the waterline. That would fit the description of 'rocket-bomb-torpedo' exactly, but technical difficulties had prevented it from becoming operational. Advanced anti-aircraft missiles, particularly *Rheintochter* (Rhine Maiden) and *Wasserfall* (Waterfall), were also under development, but they too had been held back, largely by priority on materials and manpower being given to the V-weapons, and never came into service.

Since before the outbreak of war, it had been recognised in Germany as elsewhere, that increasing speed in flight by manned aircraft would eventually be limited by the troublesome phenomena of the transonic regime, and work was put in hand with the principal objective of delaying the onset of this. The measure of success would be in enabling flight speeds to edge safely nearer to the speed of sound. Several large and impressive wind tunnels were brought into use, and by careful attention to the details of operating them, work with models had become possible up to somewhat higher speeds before the occurrence of choking than had been reached in Britain.

However, in Germany they were no nearer to finding a way of operating them throughout the transonic region. Their most significant discovery, to which Allied intelligence services had not gained access, was that sweeping the wings of aircraft backwards (or forwards) delayed to a higher speed the onset of the rise in drag that accompanied the approach to the speed of sound. The flying wing, which had been painstakingly researched by Alexander Lippisch since the late 1920s, had been given the swept-back form, to spread its lifting surface over a sufficient length in the direction of flight to provide enough longitudinal stability. This configuration came into operational use in a new form in the Messerschmitt Me 163 rocket-propelled fighter, which the Medmenham photographic interpreters had seen on the airfield at Peenemünde. This was the first aircraft to employ swept-back wings, now with the expectation that it would be able to fly at higher speed. In 1941, an early version of this aircraft had been the first to exceed 1,000kph (620mph or above 80 per cent of sonic speed at the height of the test), but the entry into service of a developed form had been delayed thereafter by dithering over its operational role and failures of organisation until too late for it to have much effect on the Allied bomber offensive.

In the excitement of learning about the advantage of using sweepback at high speed the Allied teams seem to have discounted the accompanying problems in stability and control, that were experienced with this layout at the lower speeds of take-off and landing, and under high acceleration during combat manoeuvres. These had not been fully solved by the Germans, and much work was needed in this area after the war before sweepback could become the universal feature that it is today. However, instead of the measured development that this required, a new urgency arose in the West, from the realisation that the German work would be vigorously followed up in the USSR. The scientific basis of the technology of applying sweepback had to be learnt under pressure of time.

Practically all German aircraft newly entering service and at the prototype stage near the end of the war used turbojet engines. These would be essential for a new generation of high-speed aircraft, since the propeller, with its speed of rotation combined with the forward speed, was the first part to experience the problems of transonic motion. The superiority of the turbojet over the piston engine/ propeller power plant was clearly shown in the higher performances obtained by the Arado Ar 234 bomber and the Messerschmitt Me 262 fighter, being significantly faster than contemporary propeller-driven types (the sweepback of the Me 262 wing was too small to contribute much to this, having been introduced only to correct the position of the centre of gravity when the production engines for it were heavier than those around which it had been originally designed). These aircraft were able to reach flight speeds that came close to those at which the troubles of the transonic range began. There were strict rules to avoid allowing the speed to build up in a dive, when both types became abruptly uncontrollable.

But it was found that no supersonic aircraft existed in Germany or had been planned at the time of Cleff's last visits there in 1942. Although missiles, and especially the V–2 and its intended successors, were operating at supersonic speed, work on aircraft had been sufficiently exercised in dealing with the problems of entering the transonic region. Only in the last days of the war had a contract been placed on the Siebel company of Halle near Berlin, to design a research aircraft to start the exploration of flight in the supersonic region. But it was to be rocket-propelled, so because of its limited duration of a few minutes under power, it would have to be air-launched, after being carried to operating height under a bomber. Following its flight, it was to glide down to an unpowered landing. In time, this concept would have provided basic aerodynamic information, but would not in itself have led to an operational supersonic aircraft, able to take off and fly throughout its mission under its own power, as was intended for the M.52.

8.4 Illness

A surviving docket signed by Bellamy authorises the payment of a hotel bill for Cleff to stay in Salisbury for a period of up to fourteen days at the beginning of 1945, presumably so that he could attend trials of some kind on the extensive Army ranges on Salisbury Plain. The use of his alias of 'Mr Herbert' and the notification of his presence to the Chief Constable, as required on this occasion, were however requirements that would not be needed for much longer. It is not known how Cleff reacted to the formal ending of the war with Germany on 8 May, nor to the inescapable street celebrations across London that accompanied this. But he appeared not to have sought clearance to visit his former homeland when that became possible again.

With the ending of hostilities with Japan on 15 August 1945, the Second World War came fully to an end, after nearly six years, but on 4 October, perhaps accelerated by the hectic pace of his working, Cleff was admitted to the Queen Alexandra Military Hospital at Shenley, near St Albans in Hertfordshire, diagnosed with pulmonary tuberculosis. To overcome this, it was expected that he would require three months' treatment, followed by three months' convalescence. Yet it was reported that he defied instructions that rest was part of the treatment and asked to be supplied with the means to continue his work whilst in hospital. The Commandant of the hospital was advised that, as Cleff was 'a genius', and therefore 'sensitive', he should not be obstructed in doing that.

With the ending of the war, the Military Intelligence Branch MI 19 was to be closed down in November, and so arrangements had to be made to transfer Cleff to a different jurisdiction. Major Bellamy feared that on his release from hospital, his PoW status would be reasserted, with the likelihood that he would be repatriated to Germany, which was now known to be against his will. A new round of negotiations ensued, which involved the agreement of the Home Office for him to be classified as an Enemy Alien Refugee, with the expectation that in due course he would apply to become a British citizen. The Admiralty was anxious to retain his services, so he would be appointed as a Temporary Civil Servant on its payroll, at a salary of £850pa. Meanwhile, until his release from hospital, he would continue to receive the pay for a PoW of his rank, with a supplement from the Admiralty in respect of his work for them, to a total of about £10 per month.

Cleff was declared fit for transfer to a sanatorium towards the end of January 1946. MI 9, which was handling the residual business from MI 19 after its closure, was particularly anxious that he should not go to a sanatorium that was under civil management. It might have been thought that it would be troublesome if his true identity became known, or that the security classification of his work could not be maintained with certainty in a civil establishment. However, it was found that there were no sanatoria under government management, and so he was sent for convalescence to a private one in Ventnor, on the Isle of Wight. The mild climate of that location and the fresh air from the Channel were thought to be very favourable for the recovery of consumptives. Welbourn visited him there, although he was away in Germany much of the time. He had been appointed to the Naval Intelligence Forward Interrogation Centre, newly established in Antwerp, from where he travelled widely, interviewing key persons who had been involved in developments in marine propulsion. There was particular interest in the operation of steam turbines, which the German Navy had been found to have been operating at higher rotational speeds than had been the practice in Britain. To learn about this, he contacted Karl Röder in Hanover, who had advised turbine designers at Siemens and Brückner Kanis (and incidentally had been involved before the war in arranging for Cleff to be assigned to his work in Dresden). Operating the turbine at higher speed also meant that there would have to be developments in the design of gearing to give a larger reduction ratio, where the rotation at output of the turbine had to be brought down to the much lower speed of marine propellers. In this connection, Welbourn made a point of locating Wilhelm Stoeckicht in München, who was the leading exponent of planetary epicyclic gear systems at that time.

Whilst in Germany, Welbourn took the opportunity to call at Cleff's former home at Langerich. There, it was found that his mother had taken her own life when the first Allied (British) troops arrived in the town. Although his aunt was still there, having joined his mother after his father died, the house was assigned to a Major Tapson of the 4th Battalion Royal Tank Regiment. He told Welbourn that a sergeant in US Army uniform, who had been a German Jewish refugee, had called at the house hoping to find Cleff's father, to thank him for having helped him to escape from the Nazis. There were to be others later.

On another occasion, Welbourn called on Cleff's sister in Alsace, to find that her husband had been arrested as a war criminal by the new French authorities, although it was claimed to be a case of mistaken identity. When visiting Ventnor he told Cleff about this. It was found later that he had discharged himself from the sanatorium shortly afterwards and had made his way to France to argue successfully for his brother-in-law's release. As the doctor at Ventnor had been gloomy over Cleff's prognosis, Welbourn considered this episode to have been an 'extraordinary victory of mind over matter'.

Chapter Nine

The Reckoning 1: The New Fuel

9.1 The issues

Efforts to gather information on wartime German technological developments were not followed immediately by a coordinated programme of collation and evaluation. Reports on findings in specific fields, such as aviation, were at first reviewed in a rather piecemeal fashion, to extract material needed urgently in the formation of a new baseline for development in the post-war era. This was difficult enough in the chaotic period just before, and for some time after, the end of hostilities. The division of Germany between the Allied powers into administrative zones proved to be a further obstacle to it. Eventually, a joint Air Document Research Centre was set up in London to process more systematically the material extracted by British and American teams.

Key German scientists and engineers were also brought out as and when they were located, and given protected status in the four countries. Many were employed temporarily in the relevant research establishments, where their expertise could be fully tapped over a reasonable period. But information gathered in these various ways was not uniformly shared. The greatest distrust was that which quickly grew between the Soviet Union and the Western powers, effectively cutting off any communication with the eastern sector of Germany. There were examples there where entire industrial plants, with their scientific and technical staff, and sometimes most of their workforce, were summarily removed to sites in Russia. Relief at the ending of the war was soon to be displaced by unease about the working-out of the new world order that seemed to be developing.

With the war having ended, there would soon be an accumulation of hundreds of the reports of the search teams that combed Germany for information on developments in science and engineering. Remarkably, in Britain many of these were made available freely for examination, even through larger libraries and publication via the Stationery Office. Perhaps there had been a brief period of relief that there was no longer any need to maintain the high levels of secrecy attached to intelligence gathered during the war. Claims made by PoWs could be assessed at the time of their capture only by uncertain reference to internal evidence and consistency with the testimony of other prisoners, together with facts already established and intelligence from agents and informants in Germany and the occupied countries. The protection of sources had been vital then. Now it became possible in principle to compare the information that had been reported by PoWs with the actual situations at the time of their claims, available in public documents. But there seems to have been no will to do this, rather to assign things to the past and to get on with rebuilding the world for the future.

However, when reviewing in detail the contribution of an individual such as Herbert Cleff, the question of its reliability inevitably comes into focus. Now, both parts of the picture can be seen together – the situation as it was claimed to have been when he was being questioned and how it had been found to be when the war had ended. The secret new fuel had been of concern to two of the intelligence services at Latimer, so that seems to be a suitable point at which to begin.

9.2 The new fuel

Cleff's first reference to this fuel was in connection with the steam power plant designed by the team to which he was assigned in Dresden prior to his call-up into the Army in 1939. He said that they had been given its basic properties so that the performance of the plant could be estimated if it were used there in place of the usual fuel oil, although he gave no results for that, suggesting that this was not an aspect for which he had any responsibility. But he had also heard that it had been used in an experimental U-boat, which enabled it to run when submerged, without the usual supplementary electric propulsion. This was possible because the fuel was self-contained, so that no air supply was needed to provide the oxygen for combustion. The first figure that he gave for its energy release was about nine times as great as that for petrol.

The petrol value given in this comparison was typical for the energy per unit weight of petrol alone. However, even amongst the experts, it was only Lubbock who questioned whether that would provide a valid basis for comparison with the new fuel. If the petrol was being used in a rocket engine for example, its energy could not be obtained without also supplying the oxygen required to burn it, whereas for the new fuel the oxygen was said to be already present in its composition. To allow for situations like this, it became the usual practice in rocketry to give energy release values per unit weight of all the substances supplied to the engine, including any oxidiser (alternatively, that is the same as the weight of the products of combustion leaving the engine in the exhaust). It is probably significant that Lubbock had been working on the development of a liquid-fuelled rocket engine at the time

Complete combustion of petrol requires about 3.4 times its own weight of oxygen, in addition to the weight of the fuel itself. And so to provide nine times the heat of combustion of petrol, a rocket engine would have to be supplied with petrol and oxygen to a total weight of 9 x 4.4, or about 40 times that of the new fuel. Then in this context, it might have been said that the fuel had been claimed to provide not nine but 40 times the energy per unit weight that would be obtained using petrol.

It would be more informative to compare the energy release of the new fuel with that of conventional explosives, which by definition also contain their own oxygen. Relative to the one such value given by Cleff (for dynamite), the energy of the new fuel was about 20 times as great. In any field of endeavour where serious development work had been done for many years, it was very likely that the sudden appearance of something claimed to be around 20, or more, times better would be met with plain disbelief. But it was wartime, and if there was any possibility that the enemy might have made a spectacular discovery, Cleff's claim could not be simply dismissed.

He had supplied a general form of the chemical composition of this fuel, showing that its dissociation would yield only carbon dioxide and steam in the exhaust. The leading experts in physical chemistry consulted about these claims noted that the density that he had given might correspond to that of a light hydrocarbon oil, but they found on basic principles that nothing of the composition quoted could give an energy release remotely like the figures reported (the higher densities and lower energy values he gave in later interviews would not have made them any more credible).

Cleff said that he had also encountered the fuel at a laboratory of I G Farben at a location in Austria, where it was being tested as an explosive. IGF was a huge industrial conglomerate, heavily involved in the production of synthetic fuels and chemical feedstocks from coal, employing the Fischer–Tropsch process with some variations of their own. Whittle had wondered if some new chemical combinations had been discovered during the development of this process. Cleff said that he had heard that the fuel had been derived from something with a molecular structure based on three interconnected benzene rings, but in the detailed report on his claims by Egerton, it was shown that this structure alone could not provide molecular bonds with the amount of oxygen required by the claimed overall composition. Some of the newer explosives developed between the wars indeed had a structure having a cyclical form – RDX was an example of this (*Hexogen* in Germany). Irving thought that perhaps Cleff had built on something that he had heard about this, or a liquid explosive called *Myrol* (nitro–methylene), with which I G Farben had some connection. This had been briefly considered as a potential rocket fuel, but it was not as powerful as was at first suggested, and proved to be too volatile and unpredictable for practical use.

Unfortunately, it happened that no further information could be expected from examination of the wartime activities of I G Farben. It was soon found that the records of its liaison office with the German War Ministry had been systematically destroyed in 1945. This was probably in the hope of concealing how the company had actively sponsored the rise of Nazism since 1934 and had been a prime user of slave labour in chemical plants built in conjunction with the concentration camps of the SS. As a result, the full extent of the Company's activity was never to be established with certainty.

In his memoirs, Welbourn simply states, as if it were a matter of fact, that the fuel to which Cleff referred was hydrogen peroxide, H_2O_2. This was indeed found to have been the substance used in the Walter propulsion system for experimental submarines, beginning in the mid-1930s. It would have been possible for Cleff, when he was working at Dresden and on visits to Kiel, to hear things about this, but its actual composition was protected by a high security rating.

The experimental submarine V80, of 76 tons displacement, with a new hydrodynamic shape and propulsion using peroxide fuel, had attained underwater speeds that were not even approached by Allied submarines at any time during the war. There were, nevertheless, many practical difficulties to be overcome in operating the system, and the first contract for some small patrol submarines to enter service with this new technology had been placed in 1942, not long before Cleff was captured. No boat of 1,500 tons had appeared by this time, as he had claimed, although he might have heard of something planned to follow this initial order.

Hydrogen peroxide is highly reactive and requires careful handling, but it was safe to use in strong aqueous solutions with concentrations below about 85 per cent. For Navy usage, it was given the code-name *Aurol*. It was an effective source of energy since, on contact with a catalyst, hydrogen peroxide dissociates vigorously with sufficient heat release to raise the products (a mixture of steam and oxygen) to about 600°C. Initially, these hot gases were used to drive turbines directly. But in the dissociation of peroxide, there is excess oxygen, and it was realised that at this temperature a fuel injected into the combustion chamber would ignite, giving a greater overall energy release and higher temperatures. A proportion of about one part in seven by weight of petrol or other hydrocarbon fuel would be required to utilise the available oxygen fully. Decomposition of hydrogen peroxide alone was called the 'cold' process, and when used with a fuel (ie involving combustion), the 'hot' one. The energy release per unit weight of reactants for the cold process was in practice about 400 in the units used by Cleff, and with fuels up to about 2,900, but still very far below the performance in tens of thousands that he claimed for the new fuel.

Nevertheless, hydrogen peroxide is almost certainly the best option for the origin of Cleff's statements on this topic. As he said, it looks like water, (although its density is greater rather than lower, as he claimed). Catalytic decomposition could not be properly termed 'combustion' or 'explosion', but although this was called the 'cold' process it produced a considerable temperature rise and had numerous potential applications. In a correct combination with an ordinary hydrocarbon fuel, the products could be the same as those expected from a substance with the composition $C_xH_{2x}O_{3x}$ that he reported. However, he could have arrived at this supposed composition himself, without being given any information about it, as it is self-evidently a form for which the products could be molecules of CO_2 and H_2O only, the ones to be expected from the combustion of conventional fuels.

Hydrogen peroxide was used in several other ways beside in submarine propulsion, including in the Walter rocket propulsion unit for the Me 163 interceptor fighter. Secrecy about its composition in Air Force use was maintained by giving the fuel the name *T-Stoff* (usually 80 per cent peroxide), which was initially used with a simultaneous supply of *Z-Stoff* (a solution of the catalysts sodium or potassium permanganate). Cleff might have heard something about this use of the fuel, since prior to his capture an early version of the Me 163 had reached 1,000kph for the first time in level flight, a record that although supposedly secret would be likely to have been spoken about in technical circles.

The propulsion units for the later marks of this machine used the peroxide *T-Stoff* principally as an oxidant, with a fuel code-named *C-Stoff*, based on methyl alcohol and hydrazine, N_2H_4, which introduced nitrogen into the reaction. These two components ignite spontaneously when they come into contact, by which they are said to be 'hypergolic'. It is not known how Cleff could have learnt anything directly about this combination, but when asked about a 'rocket-bomb-torpedo', that had been mentioned by other PoWs, he reported having heard of something of that description which used a propellant consisting of two fluids mixing together, and that it produced an exhaust stream with a yellowish colour. That would be a typical indication of the presence of nitrogen oxides, but the 'hot' process was not known to have been used on the weapons that fitted that description (such as the Henschel Hs 293 guided antiship missile). It has to be supposed that Cleff had possibly seen this exhaust plume somewhere in an early test of an Me 163 fighter, or was recalling something that he had heard from others.

Further support to the suggestion that it had been hydrogen peroxide that led to Cleff's figures could have been realised when it was learnt that this had been produced in quantity by a process first devised in 1936 by the German industrial chemists Riedel and Pfeiderer. The feedstock for that process is a derivative of the hydrocarbon anthracene, which indeed has a molecular structure involving three benzene rings, just as he had related. It was also the sort of product that would be supplied by a processing plant of the I G Farben group. This potential connection seems to have been missed, but nevertheless, the extraordinary values of energy release that he had reported would still remain to be explained.

Perhaps the only possibility that would account for so large a discrepancy in scale as these, was that he had mistaken the units in which they were expressed. Cleff asserted that he had merely repeated figures that he had been given, when working on the design of the steam turbine plant in Dresden. His contribution there seemed to have been in the area of mechanical design, and the energy units that he quoted, kilocalories per kilogram, were a common currency for engineering purposes at the time. It is not apparent that he had anything to do with details of the chemical thermodynamics of the system, but in that field, the basic concepts are more clearly understood when the units employed are of energy per mole, so it would be possible that the energy values recalled by Cleff had been quoted originally in this 'molar' unit.

The mole is a quantity of the substances involved, given in terms of what was then called their molecular weights, given relative to a standard, which at that time was that of the hydrogen atom. For example, taking hydrogen peroxide alone, the molecular weight is about 34. If used with an in-situ catalyst, such as platinum, where no other substances were provided, one mole of peroxide would be equivalent to 34kg. In applications, where it was diluted with water (as in 'Aurol' and *T-Stoff*) the proportion of peroxide in the overall mix would be somewhat lower, and be reduced significantly when the catalyst was supplied externally (as in *Z-Stoff*) or replaced by a hypergolic fuel (as in *C-Stoff*). A correction from molar units to mass units would thus require the energy figure to be divided by at least 34, and in some applications appreciably more.

Cleff gave three different energy values for hydrogen peroxide, without providing any connections with particular applications, so it is not practicable to evaluate fully the effect of such a change in units in each case, but in general it is clear that this could provide a correction large enough to account for the factors of 20 to 40 times noted above. If just divided by the molecular weight of hydrogen peroxide alone, the highest and lowest energy values Cleff had quoted would come to about 2,600 and 1,000 kilocal per kg, about the same order as would be expected from the 'hot' and 'cold' processes respectively.

Isaac Lubbock had supposed that the high figures for energy were probably the result of 'a combination of half-remembered things' on Cleff's part. Indeed, if there had been no occasion for him to use chemical thermodynamics since his student days, this might have included overlooking the need to allow for these different conventions for the choice of units. It is then possible that he had given the energy figures for the fuel in good faith as they had been told to him and that they were after all correct, but that he had misreported the units in which these had been expressed.

It should be pointed out here that the academic experts consulted by Lockspeiser had not simply failed to make the connection with German use of hydrogen peroxide. This was not known in Britain at the time, so it was reasonable that they had concentrated entirely on hydrocarbons as potential fuel. That the large discrepancy in energy values might have been due to a confusion over units had not been suspected, so it could be said that Cleff might have been unfairly criticised for giving the figures that he did, which he had agreed were improbable. Further his reporting about the new fuel contained other material that would stand up fairly well to comparison with what had been found by search teams scouring German facilities in the final stages of the war and immediately afterwards. He was perhaps lucky then that the energy figures had been dismissed so comprehensively on the grounds of having been scientifically implausible. They soon receded into the background and his credibility did not seem to have been seriously impaired on that account.

After his interrogations in Cairo and one at Latimer House, the Army seemed satisfied with what Cleff had said, and had required no further meetings with him. Apart from the puzzle concerning the new fuel, the one lengthy interrogation for the Navy had also been generally satisfactory. But on the reliability of matters raised in the three meetings for the RAF there had been many more concerns. In particular, there remained to review what he had claimed about developments in aircraft and projectiles and their means of propulsion.

Chapter Ten

The Reckoning 2: Projectiles and Aircraft

10.1 Athodyd propulsion

The term athodyd, a contraction of aerothermodynamic duct, was used widely in the Latimer reports. It had been coined to represent a device previously called a propulsive duct in British documents, and latterly to become more widely known as the ramjet. When referring here to this device in connection with the views given by Cleff, it will perhaps be best for consistency to use the term athodyd, while otherwise using ramjet.

Although the ramjet had been proposed in principle by the Frenchman René Lorin in 1913, no–one had succeeded in bringing it to a workable form before Helmuth Walter carried out some tests at Kiel in 1937 on a duct running in a propeller-driven air stream. However, the results of these experiments were not sufficiently encouraging to lead to practical applications at that time.

In 1941, Eugen Sänger, perhaps recalling Walter's work, proposed to develop the ramjet to propel aircraft or missiles to meet a requirement of the German Air Ministry for an anti-aircraft device able to climb to a height of 12km in two minutes, and to remain operable at this altitude for about an hour. His theoretical studies showed, as had the British ones made at that time, that a useful performance could be obtained only at high flight speeds. It is notable that he continued the range of speeds for which he calculated the performance into the supersonic regime. His first experimental tests were made with ducts mounted on ground vehicles, which helped to establish the basic theory, though the propulsive efficiency at the speeds that could be reached in that way was necessarily very low.

Sänger obtained the first results for a ramjet in flight with a duct of 500mm diameter mounted above a Dornier Do 17Z bomber aircraft, as shown in Fig 19, (Th Benecke and A. W. Quick (ed), *'History of German Guided Missiles Development*, AGARD, 1957). These flights began in March 1942, so Cleff could have heard something about them before his capture. Later tests were made with an engine of 1,500mm diameter mounted on a Dornier Do 217E aircraft at speeds up to 200m/s (450mph). It is conjectured then that these flights with Dornier aircraft were the source of the name *Do Gerät* (Do device). Although probably referring initially to the ramjet, it seems to have been used more indiscriminately later, to mean any device providing reaction propulsion.

From Fig 19 can be seen the characteristic shape of a correctly-designed subsonic ramjet. The gas dynamics that govern its operation require that the section immediately after the inlet opening should increase gradually in diameter before reaching the central cylindrical section, which is the combustion chamber. Here, the fuel is injected into the internal air stream and burnt, to provide the energy input required to obtain a propulsive force. After this, the diameter contracts again to form the nozzle, in which the flow is accelerated to form the emerging jet.

Cleff's sketches, as reproduced in all parts of Fig 8, show that he consistently drew ducts of the opposite form, with a contracting inlet and an expanding outlet. (Fig 9 was drawn by someone at Latimer, to clarify what Cleff seemed to be saying; it is not his work, but still reflects the form of the ducts that he had sketched elsewhere). It must be concluded that his sketches were expressions of his imagination, not based on any actual ramjets that he had seen, or on any understanding of the scientific basis of their operation.

He might have relied for this on recollections from his time at Dresden, where the advanced steam plant had been designed. In steam turbine practice the flow was already exceeding supersonic speeds, following the introduction by the Swedish engineer Carl de Laval of the nozzle which bears his name. In that, the steam is first accelerated in subsonic flow by a contracting section of the nozzle to the point where sonic speed is reached, after which the laws of gas dynamics require that to produce a further increase, into supersonic flow, the section has to expand again. The form of such a nozzle is known as 'convergent-divergent'.

This characteristic shape is seen in the exhaust ducts of rocket engines and is evident in the drawing of the V-2 missile in Fig 14. The high-pressure gas formed in the closed combustion chamber is expanded down to the pressure of the surrounding atmosphere, allowing high supersonic exhaust velocities to be reached if a nozzle of the correct convergent-divergent form is employed. Cleff's sketch 13 in Fig 8c shows an arrangement of this type, so he was familiar with it in some context, but it seems also to have been reflected in his representation of the duct shape for his athodyds. His use of this shape where it would not be appropriate (at least for subsonic flight) suggests that he had not really understood the mechanism by which a ramjet operated to produce propulsive thrust.

Whilst being so mistaken in the surrounding sketches, it is curious that he gave so accurate an image in Sketch 12 in Fig 8c. A projectile is shown there with two sets of axes as would be used by someone analysing its motion. One set designates the principal inertial axes of the projectile (the 'body axes'), labelling them x, y and z in the standard way (there is a minor discrepancy, where the positive direction for the z-axis is shown as upwards, where the convention is that it is positive downwards). The full lines, showing the other set, are not labelled, but they are immediately recognisable as the so-called 'wind axes', defined by the direction of the motion when it is not aligned with the body axes.

From 1938 onwards, the content of German technical journals was strictly regulated, and it seems unlikely that Cleff could have read there an account of procedures for calculating the path of projectiles, or analysis of their stability, where these axes would be relevant. Perhaps he recalled seeing this image when attending a lecture and had remembered it. He would have understood the mathematics of calculating the path, and satisfaction in that might have helped to fix the image in his memory.

Although Sänger's tests had been satisfactory, he was unable to interest the German Air Ministry or the industry in the use of ramjets. It was only in 1944 that he discovered that a consultant appointed by the Air Ministry to report on this method of propulsion had mistakenly omitted a factor of two in his performance calculations, resulting in his thrust projections being too small. The Ministry began to think that ramjets might after all have a use in air defence, and work had been started again at Göttingen on the design of ramjet propulsion for anti-aircraft missiles, but it was too late for anything to be developed before the end of the war. Cleff's expectations had not been realised – no aircraft or missiles with this method of propulsion were found by the Allied search teams.

10.2 Aircraft developments

Where there were new technologies, developed in secrecy, there would often be new terminology. In early stages, this could be misused by prisoners making reports and by interrogators and translators. There is some possibility that aircraft recorded as having athodyd power plants might actually have been powered by turbojet engines. However, the scope for that would be low, as only a small number of aircraft in that category existed in Germany prior to the date of Cleff being taken prisoner.

One photograph he said he had been shown was described as a Heinkel jet fighter aircraft. He claimed also to have seen this on an airfield, and to have spoken to a pilot who had flown it. The first turbojet-propelled aircraft to fly had in fact been a Heinkel design, the diminutive experimental He 178 of 1939, although this had not been intended to go into service. In 1942, the twin-engined He 280 was the only Heinkel turbojet aircraft flying. This would not fit Cleff's description in its original form, although the first prototype was later converted into a test vehicle for the pulse-jet engines being developed for the V-1 flying bomb. These were athodyds of a kind, although six of them were fitted, and mounted externally, rather than there being four, enclosed within the wing, as in Cleff's account. This aircraft also had a long, pointed nose with a conventional cockpit, not a transparent one in which the pilot lay prone, as he described. Any connection here therefore seems unlikely.

Another photograph described by Cleff depicted what seemed to be a version of the large Junkers/Messerschmitt mixed power-plant aircraft to which he had referred in his first interrogation. Now it was said not to need propellers for the first stages of flight, being fitted with rocket units for this purpose, to be jettisoned after use. The Germans did use this technology, in another application of Walter's peroxide rockets. But this change in what Cleff was reporting has the appearance of being a correction, as if he might have become aware that his original statement that the athodyd propulsion took over at only 75mph had no credibility. He went on to describe the aircraft as now having two fuselages, coming together at a narrow angle to join at the rear, and to weigh 50 tons. Nothing had come to light by the end of the war that might have accounted for such a strange conception.

Nor could anything be traced that would resemble the large seaplane, that Cleff claimed to have been shown in other photographs. This supposedly had a span of 72m (236ft). There was a 6-engined Blohm und Voss Bv 222 aircraft, that Eric Brown described as 'the biggest operational flying boat in the world' when he had to collect one from Norway, but this had a span of only 46m (151ft). The largest German aircraft on record was another flying boat by the same company, the Bv 238, which also had six engines but a span of 60m (197ft). Only one example had flown by the end of the war, and Cleff could not have seen a photograph of it in 1942. Both of these seaplanes were in any case powered by conventional piston engines.

It seems clear that most of what Cleff had to say concerning aircraft could have been only supposition. The discrepancies were such as to show that he could have had no direct contact with the subject-area, and knew very little about it. Even his references to known projects were vague and incidental. By contrast, accounts by *Luftwaffe* PoWs that had been included in one of the Latimer reports, spoke accurately of two aircraft that were about to come into service – a twin-jet fighter and a rocket-propelled 'flying wing' interceptor, soon to be identified as the Me 262 and the Me 163 respectively. These are shown in Fig 20.

The name *Schwalbe* (Swallow) had been associated with the Me 163 by one PoW, although it actually belonged to the Me 262 (the Me 163 was called the *Komet*). Another PoW told of the pep-talk given about these aircraft during a visit to his unit at Caen by Adolf Galland, as General of the Fighter Arm, when he had spoken of them enthusiastically. He attributed the jet fighter to Heinkel, but that was not necessarily a mistake, since at the time the He 280 was still in a contest with the Me 262 for the production contract, which was awarded to Messerschmitt shortly after. Apart from one desperate programme to produce a 'People's Fighter', too late to have any effect, these two types were amongst the last new aircraft with which the defenders were equipped. The German aircraft industry continued to pour out project proposals, of remarkable diversity, but between endemic Government mismanagement on one hand and the relentless bombing assaults of the Allies on the other, no novel advanced aircraft such as Cleff had described made their appearance. As nothing resembling them seems even to have been projected, they could only have been the product of a lively imagination.

10.3 Missiles

Welbourn went to see R. V. Jones in the summer of 1943, to hear what was known by the Scientific Intelligence arm of the Air Ministry about long-range rockets, in relation to Cleff's account of having seen the launching of one from a site in the Black Forest. He learnt that a controversy about such weapons was in progress. Opinions ranged from the prospect of missiles weighing 100 tons or more to a refusal even to believe in their existence in any form. Jones, a proponent of bringing science to bear in the business of gathering and interpreting intelligence, worked by the patient extraction of the reality from the mass of fragmented and contradictory information that came in from a multitude of different sources.

It was often necessary to resort to conjecture, but that was always to be guided by scientific principles. Objects that might be large rockets had only recently been seen for the first time in reconnaissance photographs, and the sketch of what they might be like, shown in Fig 21, represented, he said, 'the limit of British knowledge' of them at the time. When compared with the dimensions of the actual missile, shown in Fig 14, those estimated by Jones' scientific investigators had been surprisingly accurate, despite having been obtained from images about a millimetre long on photographs taken from eight miles high (the rounded shape of the nose was because these were specimens for static test-firing, so had not been fitted with the sharp nose-cone.)

In April 1943 a group of experts had been appointed to establish the nature and scale of a possible threat to Britain from long-range rockets, with D. E. (Duncan) Sandys in the chair. There was a powerful presence in this group from those who were responsible for the development of the solid-fuel rockets that were in service with British forces at the time. They established that, to carry a reasonable warhead of a few tons of explosive over a range of a few hundred miles, solid-fuel rockets would have to be multi-stage missiles, with weights at take-off of 60 to 100 tons. The one that Cleff had claimed to have seen launched, weighing 85 tons without its warhead, would provide some support to the view that long-range rockets would have to be of this size. On the other hand, he said that it used liquid fuels, a 'well-known chemical compound' for the booster stage and the new high-energy one for the main projectile.

He provided a mass of supporting detail about this missile and the facility from which it was launched, but it will be sufficient here to evaluate just one item. Cleff stated that it was propelled with an initial acceleration of 8g along its launching ramp, sloping upward at about 30°. To produce that acceleration the engines of the first stage would have to apply a thrust of 8.5 times the weight of the whole, (eight times to provide the acceleration and 0.5 to support the component of the weight of the missile on a slope of 30°). For the missile he described, this would amount to over 720 tons. Thrusts of this magnitude, well in excess of a million pounds, were not obtained until the start of the Space Age. Because of the intense noise pressures generated by the exhausts, observers of a launch of one of these large vehicles would then be kept far away, but Cleff said he had watched from a position only 25m from the edge of the launching pit. Although a practical matter of this kind had not been encountered in British experience at that time, it is surprising that the huge thrust requirement for rockets weighing 100 tons seems not to have been commented upon.

In the interrogation report in which most of the claims were recorded, the compiler expressed the moderate view that certain of the working figures given had almost certainly been 'filled in by the P/W from his own knowledge of the probabilities rather than from an actual knowledge of specific facts'. With the mathematical ability claimed for him by Welbourn, Cleff should have been able to anticipate an exercise carried out by G. I. Taylor (now a member of the Sandys committee), undertaken he said with the modest aim 'to clear my own mind, rather than to add anything to what is known'. This required the solution of a straightforward differential equation, although the skill in addressing such problems is more in formulating the equation than in its solution.

With simple, but reasonable, assumptions, Taylor's solution showed that the maximum possible range of a rocket depended principally on just two quantities – the velocity of the exhaust and the fraction of the weight at take-off which was represented by the weight of the fuel carried. There were rather strict limits to the exhaust velocity that could be used in practice, since it depended in turn on the temperature that could be tolerated in the combustion chamber. With a practicable value for this, Taylor's equation showed that a single-stage rocket could have the range necessary to reach London from German-controlled territory only if the initial fuel weight fraction was more than about 60 per cent of the whole.

A large rocket with such a high fuel fraction was hard to imagine with current solid-fuel technology, and that should perhaps have provided another reason for disposing of that option immediately. But it did not end the controversy, which is related in detail in Irving's book *The Mare's Nest*. The matter was eventually settled in favour of liquid fuel just before the first V-2 rockets arrived in London. This was the result of the accumulation of intelligence information and the heroic transmission to Britain of parts of missiles that had gone astray or had been seized by partisans from the impact points of tests on the range in Poland, before the German technicians could get there. The details were confirmed by the search teams after the war. The V-2 had a weight of only 12.7 tons at take-off, of which the liquid fuels accounted for 69 per cent, well over the estimate made by Taylor. The thrust of its engine was 25 tons, so as it was launched vertically, its initial acceleration was about 1g.

Nothing was uncovered that might point to a source for Cleff's account of the large projectile that he claimed to have seen launched, nor of the sources for the methods he used later in estimating the many values he associated with it. He said that he had once been to Peenemünde, to give advice on nozzles for high-speed fluid flow, but it is doubtful if he saw a rocket launched there, or he would have known that they were not propelled along a sloping ramp. He might have seen, or at least heard, a rocket engine on test, as he referred accurately to its 'making a tremendous screaming noise'. Perhaps he never saw a V-2 missile as such at all, since the first successful flight of one did not take place until 3 October 1942. The rocket that he described was quite unlike it – not only of much greater weight, but was shorter and wider, with a large booster stage.

It is possible however that his hosts at Peenemünde might have told him something of the history of their work without breaching strict secrecy. This work had begun in 1930, and was centred around a planned series of rockets, the *Aggregat* or A-series. From the beginning, these had all used the liquid-fuel combination of alcohol and liquid oxygen (the alcohol diluted with water to reduce the combustion temperature to a more manageable value). The A4 rocket had become the V-2 missile, but the series was planned to continue up to a large two-stage intercontinental vehicle. This was to comprise the A9, an enlarged version of the A4, probably with wings, with a booster stage, the A10. It is widely believed that the influence of Wernher von Braun, who had been with the project from 1932, had always been directed towards travel into space, for which this vehicle might have been adapted. It was recorded that after the first successful flight of an A4, he remarked that the only regrettable thing about it had been that it had landed on the wrong planet.

Cleff said that some of the details in his sketch 3 of Fig 10 were remembered from a drawing that he had seen. But this sketch does not give a correct impression of the proportions that he quoted, which are unlike the slender forms of all the Peenemünde rockets. The nearest possibility is that he might have recalled being shown a drawing of the planned A10/A9 vehicle, which was also to have a weight of 85 tons as he had quoted. An outline of the A10 booster stage of this is shown in Fig 22, where it is compared with one of Cleff's projectiles, redrawn with the dimensions that he gave shown in their correct proportions. The shapes are somewhat similar, although to make the direct comparison as shown, the scale of the one described by Cleff has had to be roughly doubled. Any connection between them is at best tenuous, and is given only because nothing else has emerged that might account for the scale of the rocket described by Cleff.

Thus, in this area also, as in all those connected with flight, no solid basis could be found for Cleff's assertions, and it must be supposed that they were all conjectural on his part. If he had heard of a project for an 85 ton rocket in 1940, say the A10/A9, he might have thought that by 1943 it could have become a reality. Thinking that rockets had to be launched along a ramp, he would realise that it had to reach a speed high enough for its fins to control its flight, before reaching the end of the ramp. The ramp would have to be long (he said about 100 metres) and its acceleration along it would have to be high (he said 8g). A recollection of having seen a drawing of the A10 vehicle might after some time have suggested that its large fins were part of a separate booster stage that would provide the thrust required for this.

He thought that the propulsion units for the projectile itself required a liquid fuel, for which he gave a weight of only 15 tons. The fuel was the secret new one that he had spoken of, but since its energy content was exceptionally high only that relatively small amount would be required. One of the interrogators present records that Cleff remarked, perhaps significantly in view of the puzzlement as to the origin of his figures, that the high energy release 'must be so, to yield the necessary power'. There is an implication here that perhaps he had started with the idea that long-range rocket projectiles had to be huge (like the A10 first stage shown in a Peenemünde drawing), and compounded that with the assumption that it had to be launched along a sloping ramp.

As he had heard that a new fuel existed with the exceptional properties he had recalled, he would not be surprised at the low fuel weight fraction that resulted. He did not have the insight of Taylor, or he would have seen that the high combustion temperatures associated with the high energy values were far beyond anything that could be withstood by known materials. When challenged about this, Cleff could offer only a facile arrangement of alternating combustion chambers cooled by air.

His motivation, in not clarifying the distinction between what he knew and what he supposed, even after he had assured Welbourn that he was ready to help towards an Allied victory, is a matter for later consideration. The arrival of the V-2 and its revelation of remarkable technical ability on the part of the Germans was probably enough to displace any recollection that Cleff had envisaged something that differed from it in almost every respect. Now the primary concerns of the military authorities were the preparations for the final assault on the territory of Germany itself, whilst the civil authorities had to deal with a new bombardment, against which there was no real defence, at a time when there had been high expectations that the war was drawing to an end.

Chapter Eleven

Post-war Life

11.1 Cleff to the Admiralty

Although on the winning side, Britain in 1946 was in a very precarious economic position. From the earliest years of the struggle, the country had mobilised its resources to bring about a state of 'total war', so that over much of the duration of nearly six years, virtually all of its means, human as well as material, were directed in one way or another towards the objective of winning it. As a result, it was now virtually bankrupt at home, whilst many of the great assets that it had previously held around the world had been dissipated. But somehow, it had to rebuild its shattered economy and return its exhausted industry to the task of restoring the international trade by which the country earned its living. A major contributor to this would have to be a rapid but controlled retrenchment in its military forces and the facilities that had been built up to support them.

When seen against this background, it is all the more notable that Cleff's services were sufficiently valued that he was able to return to the MoS and continue his work after he left hospital. But as headquarters staffing was reduced, Brigadier Blagden, to whom he reported, was transferred to the Fighting Vehicles Research and

Development Establishment (FVRDE) at Chobham, near Woking in Surrey, newly formed from several hitherto independent units. It is not clear whether Cleff moved there with him, but it seems that shortly afterwards Blagden was killed in a motorcycle accident, and the Admiralty, which had taken over responsibility for Cleff, then decided to take up his services full-time. He was transferred to the Admiralty complex at Bath where, eventually, most of the Naval Engineering activity was concentrated; though he was soon to be working with Welbourn again, as related shortly.

At this time, Cleff made the decision to apply for naturalisation in his chosen country, finally becoming a British subject on 30 March 1949, announced publicly in the London Gazette on 4 April. His Certificate gives an address in Warminster Road, Bathampton. Having to decide the name by which he would be known, he elected to be 'Peter Herbert Cleff', just reversing the order of his given names. This choice was reasonable, as Peter had been preferred by his family and friends in Germany, and later was allowed to be used by Welbourn. As his cover name in civilian life had been 'Peter Herbert', he was presumably also called Peter by acquaintances at work. Both his given names were in common use in Britain, and his surname Cleff would attract no comment, being easily taken to be one of the many regional names encountered here. His choice of name as a British citizen was not only the simplest, but one that would give no indication of his German origin.

Although there is little information in the public records on the day-to-day contributions made by Cleff during his time as a civil servant, it is apparent that for the Admiralty his work was concerned with problems in gearing. One part of this emerges in British patents in his name that were granted in the post-war years. Some of these were held jointly by him and the Admiralty, so protocol required that he would now find himself linked in a way that the former *Hauptmann* could surely never have imagined. The petitioners for the first patent are given as 'Peter Herbert Cleff and Denys Chester Ford, KCB, CBE, Vice Admiral (E), both of the Admiralty, London W1, both British citizens.'

The application for this patent (GB691734) was made in August 1949, although the complete Specification was not published until May 1953, with the title *Improvements in Instruments for Measuring the Accuracy of Profile of Gear Teeth*. Gears, like any products emerging in succession from a manufacturing process, will over time progressively depart from their ideal form, as the tooling used to produce them experiences wear in use. Regular checking is a universal procedure, so that the tooling can be changed when the profile of the product is found to have moved beyond specified limits. In the case of a pair of gears, the shapes of the teeth have to conform very accurately to the ideal theoretical shape to ensure that the correct action occurs between them as they rotate together. Further, unless the shape is accurate, stresses in the material will not be as calculated by the designer, leading to excessive wear in service and perhaps to failure. Quick and accurate methods of checking the shape are essential for such products. The usual method at that time was by use of the 'shadowgraph', in which an enlarged shadow of the gear tooth profile is projected onto a screen, where it can be compared with a similarly-enlarged outline of the correct form.

It is not necessary here to give much detail of how this is achieved in Cleff's invention, except so far as to note how it relates to the working of his mind. It will also be found later that the basic idea from this first patent is developed in some others that followed. In the explanation, as given in the patent, the reference to the involute form is to the most common geometrical shape used for gear teeth, and that to a conic section is to another shape that is much easier to generate than the involute (in this case, an ellipse is chosen). With slight abridgement, the patent states that 'The invention is based on the realisation that a mathematically correct involute gear tooth profile can be replaced with a very high degree of accuracy by a small part of a conic section, which can be generated by a simple mechanism'. It goes on to describe the device shown in Fig 23, in which the tip 15 of a tracing stylus 17 is moved over the surface of the gear tooth of which the shape is being checked. The mechanism is designed so that the deviation from the actual profile (represented by a part of the inclined ellipse 16) from the ideal form (an involute) is indicated by the dial gauge 19 shown at the right of the drawing.

The patent is unusual in containing an extensive justification of the claim, made in what Cleff described as 'complex mathematics'. It is a procedure for finding the dimensions of the particular ellipse that conforms most closely to the part of the involute that defines the ideal shape of the gear tooth. This was done by ensuring that the two curves are matched as nearly as possible at five points along the length of the tooth surface. The greatest deviation of the approximate (elliptical) curve from the correct (involute) one is claimed to be typically not more than a few millionths of an inch.

In essence, the form of the best ellipse had to be found by solving five simultaneous equations. To carry out the necessary procedure at that time would have required much labour, as the final stage involves extensive repetitive numerical work. The original development of the process, including verification of its accuracy over a series of typical examples, would have required concentrated effort over a long period. Once expressed by a specified routine, the solution would today be completed in an instant on the simplest personal computer, but the best assistance then available would have been from electro-mechanical calculators, which would probably be available in the Admiralty's engineering branch, although these could perform only the four basic operations of arithmetic.

The mechanism that generates the required elliptical curve in the device shown in Fig 23 is a version of the 4-bar chain, of which an example was shown in Fig 2. This was to have been the subject of Cleff's doctoral thesis of a decade earlier, if it had not been terminated by preparations for the approaching war. Evidently, he had continued to think about the work that he started then, and perhaps this was the subject of his spare-time work, which Welbourn had said, without explanation, might be publishable.

11.2 End game for the M.52

In the winter of 1945/46 components and sub-assemblies were being prepared at Woodley in readiness for the construction of the first prototype of the M.52 supersonic aircraft. This critical phase of its development was marked by special attention to ensuring that its final external shape would be as close as possible to the strict aerodynamic forms prescribed at the design stage. The construction of the wings provides an example of the ingenuity brought to bear by Miles throughout this project. For these, the firm had devised a novel method of construction for which a patent application was submitted under the special terms for the protection of invention during wartime. Each top and bottom skin was to be formed from a single aluminium alloy sheet, curved to a cylindrical shape with a large and constant radius. On assembly, these would be joined to the internal structure of the wing, consisting of spars and ribs in the usual manner. This structure was tapered uniformly from the wing root to the tip so as to produce the thinnest practicable thickness ratio in the finished component, as required by supersonic aerodynamic theory.

A special feature of this construction was that, with skins of cylindrical form, lines in the spanwise direction (root to tip) were straight lines. Then the internal structure could be made slightly oversize, and after having been fully assembled, could be machined to its finished size on standard machinery, very simply and accurately. The skins were then to be attached to the internal structure with flush riveting, to produce a wing that was not only very robust, but that took on the required symmetrical, thin and sharp-edged form with great fidelity. No wing of this construction had ever been built before.

The frames for the internal structure of the fuselage were similarly to be made oversize and machined to final size after assembly, for which a lathe was acquired that could accept a work-piece of sufficiently large diameter, having originally been made for finishing the wheels of locomotives. For most of its length, the fuselage was to be of constant diameter, so the skins for that part could again be formed by rolling to a constant radius. In preparation for the final assembly, correspondingly close attention was being given to the design of the jigs and fixtures required to hold the various components in position, accurately and rigidly, before they were joined together. Optical instruments were used to ensure the correct alignments for this.

Miles reported later that by February 1946, the detail design was 90 per cent completed, construction of all jigs finished and component assembly well in hand. All items required for completion were in the stores and the engine was available. It had become possible to envisage the forthcoming roll-out of the first prototype, already allocated its service airframe serial number, RT136, as illustrated in Fig 24.

At that point, a directive was received from the Ministry that the project had been cancelled and that all work on it must stop immediately.

Due to its high security classification, the existence of the project had not been made public, and secrecy was maintained until later in the year. When some details of the aircraft and news of its cancellation became known it was immediately recognised that a huge opportunity had been squandered. The uproar that accompanied questioning by the press about the termination was not assuaged when Lockspeiser gave various reasons for it at different times. This seeming evasion has helped to generate and to sustain speculation ever since. Unfortunately that has in turn perpetuated myths and misunderstandings about the project and on conspiracies over its termination that continue down to the present time.

Whilst no official record of the reason for the cancellation has come to light subsequently, it was probably due to a combination of several factors. A feeling that the M.52 project might not represent the best way to advance aeronautical knowledge at that time can be sensed in the minutes of the later meetings of the Supersonics Committee. This could not have been known to Miles, who had not been represented on the Committee, and had not even been told of its existence. There was no strong voice there, to make any direct input about progress on the project, or to correct misinformation when that arose. At that critical time, government expenditure was under the tightest control, and continuation of the programme was bound to be discussed when the Committee was asked for an opinion after Miles had submitted its estimates for the remaining costs to complete it.

Expressing his own doubts, Lockspeiser said that doing it the M.52 way could now be seen as 'putting the cart before the horse'. This was presumably a reflection of the concern felt about British work when compared with the extent of German work during the war, which was now regarded as the new benchmark of progress. There, the emphasis had been on methods of delaying the onset of the drag rise and loss of control that were being experienced on entering the transonic range. It seemed then that this must be the right approach – transonic aerodynamics should be understood and mastered fully before thoughts could be turned towards the supersonic regime. The Germans had found that the swept wing was helpful in this regard, but the British and Americans had missed the significance of it almost completely (Robert T Jones had independently proposed it in an NACA report only at the beginning of 1945). There were feverish recriminations over the British failure to appreciate something significant that German test work had verified in 1940. The use of a straight wing for the M.52 might now have seemed old-fashioned.

In June 1945, Barnes Wallis of Vickers-Armstrong Aircraft Ltd was brought onto the Committee. In aviation circles he was already famous as the inventor of the 'bouncing bomb' codenamed 'Upkeep' used to breach the dams in the Ruhr area, and the massive deep-penetration bombs 'Tallboy' and 'Grand Slam'. His prestige was high and the Committee was ready to be persuaded when Wallis suggested that data on transonic flight could be obtained more quickly, safely and comprehensively with rocket-propelled models. For instance, these could have various forms, the first ones replicating the intended shape of the M.52 and later ones employing swept wings and other new planforms such as the delta, for direct comparisons. This idea for acquiring transonic data had been suggested early in the Committee's discussions, but had been rejected as impracticable when only standard solid-propellant rockets would be available for the job. Subsequent developments in lightweight rockets, or perhaps a liquid-fuelled rocket engine based on what had been learned from experience in Germany would now make that possible. Wallis was invited to prepare a proposal for a project along these lines.

It is ironical that this project using models was in turn terminated in 1948, after committing expenditure much greater than had been requested to complete the M.52 programme. Only one successful flight had been achieved, in which a 3:10 scale model of the M.52, with a liquid-fuelled rocket engine, flew smoothly under automatic control through the transonic region to a maximum speed well beyond the speed of sound. But there were difficulties in interpreting the data from the flight, which were sent by telemetry from the model to a ground station on the Isles of Scilly. It was concluded that this method of testing was too costly and insufficiently reliable for further use.

11.3 With Welbourn again

After the hostilities in Europe came to an end, Welbourn's wartime service was due to finish also, but whilst he considered options for returning to civilian life, he was offered a role for the Admiralty, which would build on his knowledge of engineering and use of the German language. Like the other Ministries, the Admiralty was impressed with the wartime German technical progress in its field, and he was appointed to seek out their experts in maritime technology with a view to integrating their advances into British practice. Remaining in uniform, he was given freedom of movement in the parts of Europe occupied by the Western powers, with an RAF contact to assist with transport by air. His memoirs show that he was very assiduous in this, travelling widely in seeking out and questioning all the leading people and in the process acknowledging that he was himself learning much about technical fields of which he had previously little experience. By 1947 however, the political situation in Europe had hardened and the beginning of the Iron Curtain was already in place. At that time, Welbourn helped with an RN operation to smuggle out a team of eleven persons from the firm of Brückner Kanis in Dresden, which was now in the Russian zone of Germany and was about to be moved en bloc to the East.

One outcome of the Admiralty's review of its future programme was a plan to encourage the Bedford firm of W H Allen Sons & Co Ltd, which had been a significant builder of equipment for Naval purposes during the war, to move into the manufacture of steam turbines and related equipment. A contract would be offered to them, the completion of which would require substantial reorganising and modernising of their plant. The intention was to assist this by obtaining the services of certain of the leading German experts who had been contacted by Welbourn. To facilitate their interaction with the firm, it was arranged for him to be appointed temporarily to their staff, and to go to Germany to seek specifically the cooperation of Karl Röder on turbine technology and Wilhelm Stoekicht on the reduction gear that would be needed to match the fast-moving turbine to the slow rotation of a ship's propeller shaft.

It was the general practice at the time to use a pair of spur gears to bring about the speed reduction: typically by a ratio of about 10 to 1 in speed. Those used in the great ocean liners of the pre-war years were often illustrated, showing them to be major engineering products in their own right, of large size and great weight. As part of the transmission chain, they were vital components in the safe operation of the vessel. Stoekicht had specialised in epicyclic gearing, an arrangement which might be viewed approximately as a way of combining the speed reduction of two stages in one assembly. This was much more compact and lighter than the single-stage reduction gearing, and provided the additional benefit of allowing the turbine and propeller shaft to be kept in line, whereas with spur gears they were necessarily separated laterally

The involvement of the German engineers took place as planned, as both had been located in the parts of the country occupied by the western Allies. At different times they were taken in to live with Welbourn's family, Röder coming first, although he only stayed for a few months, and then Stoekicht, for a longer period, in which an Allen-Stoekicht gear department was set up at Allen's, with Welbourn as its first manager.

During this time, the Admiralty sent Cleff to work there also, and he shared an office with Welourn for a time. His own recent work had been on marine gearing, and now, apart from gaining experience in a plant where gears were to be manufactured, this posting would enable him to work up an idea that had been mentioned in the application for the patent previously described, but was not covered in the specification. It was a further consequence of the same basic principle, that a shape substantially indistinguishable from that required for gear teeth could be generated by a simple mechanism based on the 4-bar chain. Such a mechanism might then form the basis of a grinding machine, for use in the final stage of finishing the teeth. Cleff claimed that tools designed on this basis, both for grinding the profile and for checking it, would 'possess the virtue of the greatest possible simplicity, and therefore lend themselves to accurate and inexpensive manufacturing processes.' He did not complete his design of a grinding machine during his time at Allen's, although he continued to develop the idea, and it was to emerge again in his later work.

11.4 Cleff in the North

The Röder/Stoekicht project had novel features, but was of a modest scale, the turbine output being 200hp at 30,000rpm. With growing financial pressures on the Admiralty, Allen's found themselves expected to carry more of the costs, and at length the Board decided not to proceed with it. And so, in 1950, Welbourn left the firm, ended his Naval connections and moved to another engineering job in the private sector.

Although remaining on the payroll of the Admiralty, Cleff was moved to join Parson's, the famous marine turbine manufacturers, of Newcastle-upon-Tyne. This firm continued the inheritance of the steam turbine invented by Charles Parsons, which had been demonstrated for marine propulsion in the launch *Turbinia*. Widespread publicity was attracted when the launch was daringly taken at high speed on a path through the Fleet Review off Portsmouth on the occasion of Queen Victoria's Diamond Jubilee in 1897. Steam turbine propulsion was quickly adopted thereafter, both

by the Admiralty and for passenger shipping. The section joined by
Cleff was the newly-established Parson's and Marine Engineering
Turbine Research and Development Association, PAMETRADA,
at Wallsend-on-Tyne. His work was again in the area of gearing, and
his ideas on gear grinding and checking machinery soon came to the
surface there.

At the end of 1949, it had been pointed out from the Directorate of
Contracts at the Admiralty that a fee would soon be due to continue
the currency of the patent on Cleff's gear measuring device. Since
no application had been received from anyone for a license to
commercialise it, Cleff was asked if it was worth renewing. He
replied that he had realised that there was a 'technical drawback' in
the design, in that the device was to be mounted on the gear to be
measured as a reference (see Fig 23), whereas preferably it should
be positioned on a fixed reference frame, independent of the gear
(this would be because the points of contact of the ball feet of the
device are on other teeth of the gear, which would themselves have
been subject to wear, making the position of the gauge uncertain).
And so the patent would not be worth renewing without that
being corrected, but he would shortly be drafting a specification
for a gear-grinding machine, based on the same principles, that he
thought would be of greater interest.

Cleff's time at PAMETRADA was notable for the number of
patents that were obtained, now jointly in his name and that of his
new employers. It is not necessary to the narrative to examine these
in great detail, but to indicate their technical scope those that have
been identified are listed in the adjacent Table 1. It is shown there
that the novel elements in many of these British patents were further
protected by being issued in parallel in several European countries
and in the United States. The titles show that the majority were
concerned with proposals for gear-grinding machines, although
some were on gear systems themselves and on other engineering

Table 1: Patents Published in Name of P H Cleff / PAMETRADA & BSRA

British Patent	Title	Application / Publication Date	Co-applicant	Related Patents
GB678101	Improvements in or Relating to two-speed gears	1949/1952	PAMETRADA	
GB679565	Improvements in or Relating to two-speed gearing	1949/1953	PAMETRADA	US2621546
GB691734	Improvements in Instruments for Measuring the Accuracy of Profile of Gear Teeth	1949/1953	Admiralty	
GB722011	Improvements in Generating and Measuring Involute or Modified Involute Surfaces	1951/1955	PAMETRADA	
GB722030	Improvements in Generating Involute or Modified Involute surfaces	1951/1955	PAMETRADA	
GB736657	Improvements in and Relating to Means for Generating Involute Gears	1953/1955	PAMETRADA	CH356335 DE1033993 US2888784
GB741376	Improvements in and Relating to Helical Tooth Gearing	1953/1955	PAMETRADA	CH460491
GB853688	Improvements in and Relating to Flexible Shaft Couplings	1957/1960	PAMETRADA	CH42246
GB898626	Improvements in and Relating to Means for Generating Involute Gears	1959/1962	PAMETRADA	CH418784 US3060642 DE1294789
GB925321	Self-aligning Journal Bearings	1961/1966	PAMETRADA	CH401598 US3266855
GB936754	Improvements in and relating to Flexible Pipe Joints	1961/1963	British Ship Research Association	
GB969320	Improvements in and Relating to Means for Generating Involute Gears		PAMETRADA	CH416272 DE1294786 US3091059
GB1070651	Improvements to and Relating to Planetary Gears particularly for Ship Propulsion	1965/1967	PAMETRADA	CH440010 DE1231489 NL6502315 SE310825
GB1104023	Improvements to and Relating to Planetary Gears	1964/1968	PAMETRADA	US3327555 CH441907 NL6503403 SE319053
GB1116575	Improvements in and relating to change speed gears	1965/1968	PAMETRADA	US3352177 FR1491699 NL6611328 US3320584

components, giving some indication of the continuing fertility of his inventiveness.

It seems that by this stage Cleff had overcome his difficulties with social relationships, for on 16 May 1953, when he was 41, he married Winifred Isobel Bulman of Gosforth. She was then a widow of age 42, and Director of several companies. They lived first in Alnmouth and then settled in the Westfield area in Newcastle. Welbourn, who visited them later, reports that 'Freda' had been a very supportive partner.

In 1964, Cleff set up his own company, Precision Kinematics (Gears & Mechanisms), with his wife as co-Director. Its main activity seems to have been the preparation of the three further patents for gear-grinding machinery listed in Table 2.

For these Cleff departed from his previous method, of using mechanisms based on the 4-bar chain to generate surfaces that very closely approximated the ideal involute form. His new designs were to generate the involute directly, based on the defining geometrical principle that this curve would be traced by a point on a taut cord unwinding from a base cylinder. An illustration of the application of this principle to the generation of gear tooth forms is given in Fig 25. It seemed more straightforward to design a machine employing this principle, since the edge of the grinding tool used to produce the finished surface of a gear tooth is then required only to move at a constant rate along a straight path as the gear blank revolves. However, the outlines given in Cleff's patents indicate that there were many complications in producing a satisfactory machine to do this in practice.

The Company was taken over in 1969, although continuing to trade under its original name, becoming a subsidiary company of R & W Hawthorn, Leslie & Co with works on Gibb Street, Newcastle. Its role was that of 'Consulting Engineers with special reference to the problems associated with gearing'. It made a small profit at first,

Table 2: Patents Published in Name of P H Cleff/Precision Kinematics

British Patent	Title	Application/ Publication Date	Co-applicant	Related Patents
GB1209051	Improvements in and Relating to Means for Generating Involute Gears	1967/1970	Precision Kinematics (Gears & Mechanisms) Ltd	CH480904 FR1605088 US3499252
GB1217647	Improvements to and Relating to Means for Generating Internal and External Involute and Non-involute Gears	1967/1970	Precision Kinematics (Gears & Mechanisms) Ltd	CH49091 DE1652795 FR1605087 US490919
GB1219081	Improvements to and Relating to Means for Generating Internal and External Involute and Non-involute Gears	1967/1971	Precision Kinematics (Gears & Mechanisms) Ltd	

but with increasing losses later, it ceased trading in 1975 and was moved to a holding company at a London base in 1977, before being dissolved in 1979.

11.5 Closure

Welbourn reports that Cleff's final attempt to produce a novel gear-grinding machine was made in conjunction with the long-standing Manchester firm of Craven Bros, which specialised in heavy machine tool manufacture. Details of this project are sketchy, although it appears to have been supported by a grant from the National Research Development Corporation, a body set up to encourage research activity in British industry. But it seems that the project was terminated when it was concluded that there had been a basic flaw in the way that the concept was to be realised in the design, bringing to an end a quest that had preoccupied Cleff for almost 30 years.

His last active work was as a private consultant on marine gearing, commissioned by shipping companies to travel out to wherever one of their vessels was in trouble with that component, to give advice on how it should be dealt with, on the basis of a personal examination on the spot. His expertise was widely valued, and this was a very successful business.

Cleff was recorded as only 'semi-retired' when his life came to an accidental end in 1991, at the age of 80. He died in The Royal Victoria Infirmary of burns suffered in his apartment, then in the Jesmond area of Newcastle. Evidence was given at the inquest that a fire had started in the bedroom, where he was found by the emergency services. He was known to be a heavy smoker and a cigarette lighter was found beside the bed. As he had also been taking medication to assist with sleeping, it was concluded that the most likely cause of fire had been a burning cigarette falling unnoticed onto the bedding.

An item among Cleff's effects was his father's passport, which he must have retrieved when making his one visit home in 1946. Welbourn reports that the only visa it contained was for travel to Amsterdam, where the family's company was known to have had customers. He suspected that these business trips were used in some way to help German Jews on to the first stage of escape from the increasing restrictions imposed under the Nazi regime. Although Cleff had resolutely detached himself from connections with his earlier life, it is readily understood how he would value this memento of the father whom he had greatly admired.

Chapter Twelve

The Benefit of the Doubt

12.1 Life and times

Most aspects of Herbert Cleff's life have now been brought together, so that his actions and the motivation for them may be considered. With the perspective of the whole, it could be said that his character had not developed normally in some respects. Comments were made on this throughout his time in British hands, by the interrogators and the psychologists who interviewed him at the Centres in Cairo and Latimer House, by Dr Esther Welbourn and by the consultant Henry Yellowlees to whom he was referred later. Although he was over 30 at the time, tall and lean and of good bearing, all of them remarked upon his immaturity. Yet Donald Welbourn, who had the greatest opportunity to observe him in everyday, including domestic, circumstances, noted that he could be charming and was considered to be attractive to women. Those who continued to correspond with him after his capture had evidently found him so, on the basis of their earlier acquaintances with him in Germany.

There has to be some uncertainty in interpreting Cleff's side of the wartime correspondence. This had to be conducted under great constraint, in the knowledge that every word would be read by strangers – the censors on both sides. This would be inhibiting for many, arguably more so for men, who are widely believed to be unable to express themselves in terms of intimacy in the best of circumstances. Cleff would constantly be aware also that almost anything that he could say about his situation must be fictitious, since when he wrote ostensibly from 'Camp 1', he was actually at the Latimer interrogation centre and when from 'Camp 7', he could have been in a flat in London or even at a desk at the core of the British military establishment, living under an assumed name. It was natural that from time to time his mother would ask how he was occupying himself, and to this he would reply only that he was 'busy', or would ignore the question altogether.

It would not be surprising if he were continually unsettled by these circumstances, particularly when writing to those in his homeland, the persons who knew him best. It would be especially troubling for him to deceive them about his activities, but also there would be the constant fear that they would learn that he had betrayed their country, despite the argument that what he did would be in their best interests in the long run. His vacillation about his engagement to Eli, of which she wrote so enthusiastically, might well have arisen from thoughts about what would happen after the war. She would surely expect them to be married as soon as he was able to return home. Although it was a common occurrence later (as it had been after World War One) that participants would never discuss their wartime experiences, it must have seemed to Cleff that an intention to keep his wife in ignorance of his defection could not be a satisfactory basis for a marriage. Yet if Eli learned of it, she, who had worked to the point of exhaustion in the only way open to her to help in keeping her country running, would surely despise him for his abandonment of it.

It was curious that the one item he chose to be sent on to him, when his trunk turned up long after his capture, had been his

Panzer uniform. He might not have wanted his family to keep that memento of his service to his country, or perhaps it represented to him some evidence of continuity with the past, when all else was being severed. He was facing the likelihood that he would have to take on a new identity permanently, with nothing of his former self remaining except his capacity to work.

He was known to be out of sympathy with his mother, on the grounds of her support for the cause of Nazism, but it seems that she had fulfilled all that he could have wished from a concerned parent after his capture. Following the death of his father, he became head of the family under the conventions of the time, adding respect for his new status to any reluctance his mother may have felt to criticise him when he was a prisoner in unknown circumstances. Perhaps in turn he felt that he was no longer under any obligation to give an account of himself to her. But it remains a matter of opinion whether any of this could justify his treatment of Eli, to whom he had allowed himself, as far as the situation would permit, to become engaged to be married, and then asked to be released from that. Reading the last despairing entreaties of these two women (surely the key persons in his life up to that point), it is hard to condone the manner of his terminating his contacts with them, just by no longer replying to their letters.

Some of those required to assess Cleff's state of mind noted evidence of traits that they considered to be more pathological. The report of Lieutenant Colonel Dicks, the Psychiatric Specialist at Latimer House, reproduced earlier as Fig 3, is particularly striking. He appears to have found it very significant that Cleff was 'content to sit alone in his room in this camp doing complicated integral calculus, covering pages and pages with formulae and technical drawings of incredible neatness'. This behaviour he considered to be 'obsessive', a term with clinical meaning in psychiatry, suggesting to Dicks that Cleff was 'a kind of calculating machine', likened to Dr Frankenstein, 'a morbid genius very close to insanity by ordinary standards'. But to a professional engineer, this judgment would seem outrageously hyperbolic.

The intensity of Cleff's application would not seem far beyond the level of working activity experienced at a time of great urgency in practice. In the circumstances of his capture, it was perhaps even a sensible means of occupying his time, doing things that interested him and fending off the stultifying boredom of a prisoner's day. Welbourn, a professional engineer himself, seemed to think little of it at the time.

However, when Cleff was working in the Fighting Vehicles section, his way of working was again considered excessive, even by Welbourn, who now thought that it might soon lead to a breakdown. The consultant psychiatrist Yellowlees, to whom Cleff was referred, also focused on his working activity, but suggested that this was pursued so relentlessly because it was the only aspect of life in which he could now feel secure. The primary difficulty was his inability and lack of opportunity to engage in any kind of social interaction. Dr Esther Welbourn, who had observed Cleff as a guest in their household, also identified social isolation as something that was seriously constraining his life. This deficiency had been noted by Dicks, but was thought by him to be a symptom of his obsession, rather than a cause.

Despite his listening patiently to advice from these experts, there is no evidence that Cleff took any action to create a social element on his life. Both Dicks and Yellowlees reported that he was well aware that this was an important factor of life for most people, but his continued lack of initiative in this area perhaps indicates that for him it had been absent for so long that he felt content to be without it.

Dicks reported that the obsession with mechanics that he perceived in Cleff had begun at the age of four. Psychiatrists often look for experiences in childhood that might account for difficulties in later life, and this impression must have emerged during questions about his early experiences. However, many engineers of that generation would have said that they began making things with parts of the famous construction set Meccano at around that age, and in later life regarded it as significant in the development of a spatial awareness and an attraction towards their chosen career. A reference by Cleff to something similar arising in his early life might have led Dicks to attach too much significance to it.

There seems to be no evidence that Cleff's childhood had been an unhappy one. He was not an only child, and was fond of his older sister and especially his younger brother. The family was prosperous, and was likely to have a good circle of friends and to entertain at home. Middle-class households of the time were generally strictly ordered, but he made no reference at any time to either parent having been domineering, or that he was ever treated badly in any way. He spoke affectionately of his father, and admired particularly his efforts to protect Jewish employees of his firm from the persecution of the Nazi regime. As a student, he had himself risked being penalised by not joining societies organised by the Party, but had found that there were sponsors among the senior academics who had ways of circumventing that. He would perhaps have been concerned that his mother, and later his sister, were Party supporters, but that might be thought to show that his family was a tolerant one in which widely-differing views could be accommodated. Overall, there is no evidence strong enough to suggest that his state of mind could have been destabilised by lasting effects of events in his early life.

Cleff's accounts of his experiences as a young man are brief and refer mainly to aspects of his industrial training and his first job in Dresden. Nothing is said about friendships or early romantic attachments, although the messages received from women friends via the Red Cross during the war indicate that there must have been some. Regrettably, it is not known how or where he met Eli, although she was about twelve years younger, so that must have been after his student days. It is noted that in their wartime correspondence, the initiative is invariably hers, and his response to her suggestions that their relationship should be formalised was largely one of reluctant acquiescence rather than enthusiasm.

Nothing is known about Cleff's experiences in military service beyond what he related himself. His accounts of the various places where this had taken him are internally consistent and accord well enough with the history of the early German campaigns in Western Europe and in the Eastern Sector up to the point of his posting to North Africa. German authorities have been unable to trace any records of his service, or the circumstances of his Iron Cross award, but point out that a high proportion of the relevant documentation was known to have been destroyed during the Allied bombing campaign. This happened to a lesser extent with British documentation also, when part of the World War One military records were amongst those lost or damaged by fire and water during the 'Blitz' on London in 1940/41, before they were moved to locations thought to be safer.

All of Cleff's own references to military service are on professional matters only. Of his friendships or other relations during this time there is practically no information. He enquired once of Eli whether she had news of 'Mölders and Hellerberg', seemingly mutual friends who were now away on military service (it was one of these, when home on leave, who had mentioned to her the arrangements for proxy marriages). In one of her letters, his mother referred to an incident which had caused her concern 'when he was in the *Wehrmacht*', but with no other references to that, there is no basis for speculation as to its nature.

In his civilian life in Britain, Cleff's ways were seen mainly through his involvement with Welbourn and his family, with whom he lived for some time and kept contact later. He must have shown some sterling qualities, as he was invited to become godfather to their son Hugh, although there are no references to how he exercised that role, beyond having brought the boy an air-rifle at the age of ten. His own family were likely to have been Lutheran, but there is nothing to indicate what belief, if any, he might have held in later life. In her last message to him, his mother's reference to his 'keeping the faith' could have been as much one to the Nazi creed that she supported as to any religious conviction.

Over much of the time, the Welbourn household had a succession of *'Haustöchter'*, the equivalent of 'au pairs', young women from Germany and Switzerland, who were preferred because of Welbourn's fluency with the language. Cleff seems not to have reacted to their presence at all, although that might have been because he thought that to do so would be to take an improper advantage of the situation. A rare photograph of Cleff with the *Haustochter* Eva Roegg is shown in Fig 26, the very image of mutual indifference. In what manner the pattern of his withdrawal was broken is not known.

A social side to Cleff's life had somehow developed by his 40s, since at that time he married Winifred Bulman. Nothing is said about the circumstances of their meeting, but she was a businesswoman, at the time a Director of three companies, and probably another who found her work absorbing. Welbourn noted that their marriage was a successful one. Cleff continued an active professional life, so it appears that they found some of their compatibility in making sufficient room for continuation of their respective work patterns.

12.2 Welborn and Whittle

The puzzle at the centre of Cleff's story is how a Prisoner of War could have worked so powerfully on the minds of his captors that he was released, in the middle of a war, to live independently as a civil servant, placed at the centre of his former enemy's organisations for the development of military equipment.

His reports of experiences in these areas prior to his capture seem to have been sufficiently consistent with what was already known as to be generally accepted, without causing much comment beyond a favourable one from the Navy engineering branch on the novel nature and high quality of German work. The parts of his reporting that referred to the new fuel and consequent applications to propulsion of submarines, aircraft and long-range missiles were received with more scepticism. This material would have taken its due place with all the rest in the flow of information by which the intelligence services monitored technical advances on the part of the enemy, but that was always work-in-hand, within a continually-unfolding process.

There would be new arrivals at Latimer with later material, by which the Interrogating Officers would hope to keep their assessments up to date. It is probable that Cleff would soon have had to make room for these, perhaps being moved on to an ordinary PoW camp in the summer of 1943. If so, he would most likely have had to wait out another two years of war in idleness, and probably face a frustrating delay after that, before finally being repatriated to Germany. There would have been nothing particular to differentiate him from the mass of other prisoners following a similar course.

It is clear that the exceptional turn of events that happened instead could not have occurred without the initial advocacy and the continued support and active sponsorship of Donald Welbourn. He formed a high opinion of Cleff's intellect and capabilities from the time of their earliest contacts in March 1943. There is little to be found in the reports from Cairo and the first interviews by Army interrogators there to indicate more than the competence to be expected of a tank engineering specialist. But the interrogation by Navy officers that followed, in which Cleff reported advanced work in another field, now of marine propulsion, seems already to have convinced Welbourn that he had both wider capabilities and more information that might be recovered. The daily contact that he sought and was granted enabled him to discuss engineering matters with Cleff at length, giving him the best opportunities of any to assess his abilities as an engineer. Then the wider-ranging discussions that took place between them would have revealed more of Cleff's intellect generally, whilst also disclosing the possibility that he might be prepared to assist British work towards bringing the war to an earlier end.

Once that had been agreed, Welbourn went to some lengths to secure a working position in technical development for Cleff. This had eventually taken place within the Ministry of Supply and the Admiralty, and he continued subsequently to sponsor him in various ways for at least a decade after the end of the war. Although with occasional minor caveats, Welbourn's generally high opinion of him remained. He described him at various points as 'first and foremost an original designer of great ability', 'certainly the most original kinematician of his generation' and 'probably the most brilliant all-round engineer I have ever known'. He particularly admired Cleff's practical abilities in combination with a theoretical background, recommending him to the MoS as 'a first-class practical engineer with a real mastery of the higher mathematics' and commenting on his last work as a consultant on gear problems with 'what made him an unsurpassable advisor was his theoretical understanding of what was known about gears, coupled with his ability to take scraper and file and personally do the work of a skilled fitter'. (This perhaps reflects comments made by Welbourn in his autobiography, that his own Cambridge degree course had been aimed exclusively at developing capabilities in theoretical aspects, so that when he first worked in industry after the war, he found that he could contribute virtually nothing of practical value). Cleff also made a good impression elsewhere. When the Admiralty wished to retain his services after the end of the war, he was said there to have become 'the cleverest gear and gear-cutting machinery designer in the world'.

Welbourn sought opinions outside the camp at Latimer from various significant figures, amongst whom was Frank Whittle. He too was impressed by what he perceived to be Cleff's capability, and eagerly took in the information that he brought on German gas turbine and ramjet engines and applications to missile and aircraft propulsion. Whittle's set of mind was always forward-looking, so he was likely to believe in the reality of things that were within reach of another imagination that stretched well ahead of present capability. This was to have significant consequences when Whittle was invited to be one of the group of specialists that later became the Supersonics Committee.

Ben Lockspeiser, Director of Scientific Research at the MAP, had been roused into immediate action on receiving the first of the intelligence reports on Cleff's disclosures. The people he called to the first meeting included such luminaries as Profesdor Sir Bennett Melvill Jones, Professor of Aeronautical Engineering at Cambridge and Chairman of the independent Aeronautical Research Committee, and Professor G. I. (Geoffrey) Taylor, Director of the Cavendish Laboratory. At their next meeting, only a month later, they were joined by other experts from the Aerodynamics Departments at RAE and NPL, and proceeded to consider all three of the reports then available about Cleff, the last one made after he had decided to collaborate.

The members of this group, although heavily committed at this stage of the war, were sufficiently convinced of the significance of these reports to agree to become a standing committee, meeting monthly thereafter. They formulated a modest programme of work, to reconsider the ramjet as a means of propulsion at high speed and to explore ways of obtaining aerodynamic data in the transonic speed range. However, by the eighth meeting, they had reached the momentous decision to recommend the MAP to commission the construction of the manned supersonic research aircraft that became the Miles M.52 project. This adventurous course of action was to take a place in the history of aviation. It had unquestionably been influenced strongly by the staunch support of Frank Whittle. He assured the Committee that personally he 'did not doubt' the existence of the German supersonic aircraft that Cleff had described. Moreover, he considered that providing the power to propel an experimental aircraft in this speed range 'involved no serious problem'. Tests were already in hand at Power Jets on what he had called 'thrust augmenters', which introduced the original concepts of by-pass flow and additional fuel burning or 'reheat'. These would provide a large increase in thrust beyond that of a basic turbojet engine and enable it to operate increasingly like a ramjet as the forward speed increased, due to a growing contribution of ram compression to the pressure rise required to run such an engine.

The Committee could scarcely be unimpressed when the very inventor of the jet engine described the prospective availability of this advanced power plant. It promised not only to enable an experimental aircraft to reach supersonic speeds, but also allow it to take off and land in the familiar way and climb and descend in between as required by a normal test schedule. The alternative of using rocket propulsion could not have provided a sufficient flight time for this, due to the very high fuel consumption incurred. It was hoped that this project would allow Britain to catch up rapidly with the German developments in high–speed aeronautics that Cleff had outlined.

12.3 On credibility

It can be seen in Chapter 10 that enquiries about German wartime activity had shown as early as 1945 that most of Cleff's reporting in the areas of missile and aircraft development was without foundation, but the Supersonics Committee's actions in 1943 must here be reviewed without recourse to hindsight. At the first meetings, it was concluded that Cleff was mistaken about the new high-energy fuel, and that was set aside on the grounds of being scientifically implausible. However, that could not be said with certainty at that time about his claims concerning missiles and aircraft.

This was when there was much anxiety about the possibility of attacks on British cities by long-range missiles. There was evidence that work was in progress on these, but there was fierce disagreement amongst experts about the technology that might be used for them. This turned largely on the type of fuel that could be employed, which greatly affected the estimated size and weight of the projectiles, ranging up to monsters of 100 tons, based on experience with solid fuel rockets. Cleff's claim to have seen the launch of a two-stage projectile of 85 tons weight did nothing to help settle the issue, as this was said to use a liquid fuel for the booster stage and his now discredited secret fuel for the second stage. The dispute rumbled on for more than a year, to be resolved eventually by firm evidence that the German projectile actually used (the A4 or V-2) was liquid-fuelled and weighed only about 13 tons (although it must be said, in fairness to the advisory committee, that the warhead of 1 ton was much smaller than had been expected).

A moment's calculation, to find that the booster of Cleff's reported projectile would have to provide over 700 tons of thrust, and reflection on his claim of having stood 25 metres to the side of the launching pit as it was fired, would surely have challenged, if not settled, the credibility of that part of his narrative. There is a minute that asks for intelligence to be gathered about possible activity in the region of Sagan, in Silesia, which Cleff had named as another site where large projectiles were being tested, although it seems that there had been other hints of this, so that part of his evidence was probably correct. But it seems that nothing was done to check the site he claimed to have visited in the Black Forest, which was within the range of photographic reconnaissance aircraft. These aircraft had surveyed the former Zeppelin works at Friedrichshafen, not far away at the end of Lake Constance, and that had been duly bombed.

References by intelligence sources to the *Do Gerät* might have allowed enough credence to be given to Cleff's claims about athodyds to justify the review of the 1940 assessment of ramjets and the modest experimental programme instituted by the Committee. It was not known then that the German Air Ministry had begun the phasing-out of work on piston aero-engines (ending it altogether at BMW) in favour of bringing turbojet engines up to production standard. But there was already sound evidence from prisoners and other sources about the existence of experimental and probably prototype aircraft with rocket and turbojet propulsion. The performance credited to these was sufficiently disturbing, but the strongest reaction was caused by Cleff's report of the existence of German supersonic aircraft. A claimed maximum speed of 1,800kph (1,120mph, although the figure given to his Committee by Lockspeiser was 1,000 mph) would be three times that of front-line fighters of the time, and at high altitude nearly 70 per cent faster than the speed of sound.

To act on this, the Committee seemed to need no more justification than the observation of their Chairman that if the Germans had solved the problems attending supersonic flight, they were 'years ahead of Great Britain and the USA'. There had been no discussion of what strategic advantage the enemy might gain from it. Increased speed had always given an advantage in the past, but the differential had never been so large. The immediate concern would be that high-speed aircraft would enable the enemy to intercept more effectively the Allied bomber force that was at the moment the principal weapon that could be deployed against him. Certainly, there would be a distinct benefit in being able to gain height much more quickly than before, and so to get into an advantageous position. But if maintained, too great a speed advantage would leave insufficient time after coming within range of a target aircraft to aim and fire accurately before having passed it. Then, since the radius of turn was proportional to the square of the speed, it might be so large as to make it impossible in practice to return and attack the same target again. And so, while certainly having advantage from such high speeds, pilots would probably find it necessary to slow down in the attack phase to make effective interceptions, becoming more vulnerable again to defensive measures. At night, the final stage of an interception with the aid of airborne radar had been found to require creeping up to the target at a very small speed differential. It would be expected that the Committee would at least have instituted studies of such operational matters before proceeding, but that seemingly was not considered.

This is not to say that sceptical thoughts about other factors never arose at the Committee. In a note passed from Christopher Lock to Ernest Relf, the two representatives of the NPL Aerodynamics Department, it is observed that previously they had thought that 'these supersonic speeds were quite out of the question', largely because of the rapidly-increasing drag already being experienced as speeds began to approach transonic speed, and he wondered why the Committee's view now disagreed with that. But when this was put to Whittle, he had correctly pointed out to them that work in Germany and Italy had already been well ahead of British work in this area before the war, and so it would be 'dangerous to assume' that they had not now made discoveries that had not been foreseen. This was an argument that would be difficult to counter.

There were also comments received from Theodore von Kármán, of the California Institute of Technology, who had made important advances in the analysis of supersonic flow before the war and was regarded as the foremost expert on the field in the USA. As an advisor to the Army there, he had been asked to comment on British intelligence reports that had been shared with the US authorities. He had seen those concerning Cleff, which he analysed paragraph by paragraph, but concerning the claims about a supersonic aircraft, he remarked only that the quoted performance was 'improbable', scarcely a sceptical warning.

It had been advised within the intelligence reports themselves that information given by Cleff should be treated with caution. In the first report of April 1943, after his arrival in the UK, even Welbourn conceded that he was 'apt to draw on his imagination on subjects of which his knowledge is limited and where he can see the possible development of certain scientific discoveries'. This is a recurrent theme.

In the report on his interrogation about naval matters of 10 May, it is remarked that 'at times it is somewhat difficult to assess when he is talking from his own experience and when he is talking theoretically'. And in the aeronautical interrogation of 19 May, that certain information had been 'almost certainly filled in by the P/W from his own knowledge of the probabilities rather than from an actual knowledge of specific facts'. Concerning his report on the long-range projectile and aircraft developments, it is warned that his statements 'have included certain calculations of his own. Having been told that supersonic flight has been achieved, he believes that fact. He has no definite knowledge on the subject however, and his statements in this connection have been based only on hearsay'.

Bearing in mind that all of these reports, including the warnings, had been circulated to members of the Supersonics Committee, it is easy to feel that they had been unduly credulous in their reactions to Cleff's claims. It is remarkable, for instance, that they seemed not to have enquired from the Air Ministry's own expert on scientific intelligence, Dr R. V. Jones, whether any corroborative evidence about supersonic aircraft had been received from other sources known to him. However, a more generous view would be that they had merely accepted the overall message, which was coming from others as well as Cleff, that German work in aerodynamics was more advanced than had previously been suspected.

Amongst the members was G. I. Taylor, whose work over time had shown his judgment to be invariably sound. It was noted earlier how he had put the discussion on possible long-range missiles into perspective by an elegantly simple piece of analysis. Amongst many relevant accomplishments, he had published in 1932 a critique of Ackeret's pioneering work on the characteristics of wings in supersonic flight and he had developed with his research assistants Stanley Hooker and James Maccoll, later famous contributors in their own right, a method of calculating the supersonic flow over bodies of conical shape that allowed their drag to be calculated. He had been the only British contributor invited to the famous Volta Conference on high-speed aerodynamics at Rome in 1935, which included discussion of papers contributed on early transonic flow from the American Eastman Jacobs and on supersonic flow from the German Adolf Busemann, among other leading figures. He was better placed than anyone in Britain to judge whether supersonic flight might now have come within reach. Perhaps he too was impressed when no less a figure than Frank Whittle had been enthusiastically supportive of the idea and in particular had shown the Committee that he had conceived a new variant of the turbojet engine that would provide the thrust that would be needed.

Although the project that they endorsed, to create a supersonic research aircraft, was eventually to be summarily cut short, later studies would show that it had been soundly based. In principle, the Germans could also have assimilated all the information brought to bear in the design by Miles, although the bold imagination shown by the team there would have been hard to replicate. It could not be dismissed in 1943 that the Germans might have embarked on a project resembling that of the M.52.

Cleff was totally unaware of the M.52 project or the part his claims had made in bringing it into being. Whilst it was getting under way, he was seemingly giving satisfaction in his work at the Ministry of Supply. Concerns about his overworking eventually led to consultation with the psychiatrist Yellowlees, who concluded his report with an offer to go outside his professional remit and to meet informally with Cleff occasionally to play chess. The charm of his presence was evidently not diminished.

The claims made by Cleff could not be tested thoroughly until the real situation became clearer at the end of the war. The Mission headed by the leading aeronautical engineer Roy Fedden submitted its detailed Final Report on German technology to MAP in 1945, supported by a major exhibition at Farnborough of items of significant service and research equipment that had been brought back. There was keen interest in this material from individuals in the firms and establishments, but Fedden noted that the 'senior authorities' who came showed little enthusiasm. He said afterwards that their attitude had been "What are you so excited about? We've won the War, haven't we?" By then many others felt little incentive to look back, and Cleff received the benefit of the doubt by default.

Chapter Thirteen

The Enigma of Herbert Peter Cleff

13.1 Motivation

It has been seen that there was a sharp contrast between evidence given by Cleff about matters on which he had worked himself – tank engineering and ship power plant – and that on areas like missile and aircraft technology, of which he had no direct experience. He had presented his information on those in terms implying personal acquaintance, but he seems not to have been questioned deeply about that. Disbelief over what he had said about the new fuel, and his apparent vacillation, in giving lower energy figures when he saw how his first one was received, seem not to have discredited his claims on other things, as this topic was quickly dropped. It can now be seen that in any case, he had probably simply misunderstood the units in which these figures had originally been given to him. If so, they were perhaps correct and he had reported them in good faith.

Later information was to show that his claims about missiles and aircraft were not only without any foundation, but were also wildly extravagant. Although this could not have been fully known at the time, it is to be wondered that more attention was not given to inconsistencies shown up by internal evidence within the claims themselves. A prime example of this is the account Cleff gave of the large projectile that he claimed to have seen launched from a site on the Lettstädter Höhe, in the Black Forest. Several improbable aspects concerning the projectile have been brought out earlier, where making a judgment on their credibility tended to require some knowledge of technical factors. But references here to some others might invite the reader to consider whether or not it was curious that they had not caused any comment at the time, even from those without any specialist knowledge.

For instance, Cleff gave the map reference location of the alleged test site to the nearest second of arc in latitude and longitude. This required a set of six numbers to be remembered, but no-one seems to have asked how he came to do that so precisely. The location was, and is, heavily wooded and a very popular region for hiking. It would not be unreasonable to conjecture that Cleff had visited it for this purpose in younger days, and if with an organised party, there could have been an instruction to commit the map reference to memory as a safety measure. Even so, the precision of the reference is surprising – no hiker would have the equipment to place his location within one second of arc. A simple calculation would have shown that at this latitude it would define a region on the ground with dimensions of about 20m x 30m. He went on to describe, and illustrate with sketches, a gigantic launching pit at this position, of such dimensions that would have required the removal of some 500,000 cubic metres of soil and rock, weighing well over a million tons. It was then to be lined with 'sheets of heat-resisting steel'.

Then, the pit was covered when not in use by a sliding roof of overlapping plates, which was said to be 'wonderfully camouflaged'. He was not asked how this moveable roof for something 120m long and 50/60m wide was hidden in an area of unbroken pine forests that extended for many kilometres around the specified point in all directions. It could also have been questioned that projectiles weighing many tens of tons would be fired from this beauty-spot, with the attendant fire hazard, or be directed towards a region like Lake Constance, the shores of which were already well-populated areas, and which formed part of the border with neutral Switzerland.

Although nothing resembling the launching pit Cleff described was known up to the time of his capture, plans had begun for the construction of a massive underground installation for the launching of A4 missiles from a site near Watten in north-western France. With main-line rail connections to production centres, this would include bunkers holding many rockets, with fuel storage and its own liquid-oxygen plants, to enable a practically continuous assault to be mounted against targets in England. If he had heard a rumour about this project, either before being captured or from a fellow-prisoner afterwards, Cleff might have based his conjectures on an impression of the huge scale that would be required for that. (The idea was to become obsolete later. Inevitably, something so conspicuous was soon observed whilst under construction and was heavily attacked from the air, but by then the German engineers had realised that missiles could be fired from mobile launch vehicles that were almost undetectable, and there were no attempts to rebuild it).

Although his claims were undoubtedly exaggerated, in advancing them Cliff does not seem to have adopted the bombastic stance attributed to some prisoners, asserting that anything German must in principle be superior to anything fielded by the Allies. Rather, reading about these claims being given in such a matter-of-fact way, the impression is almost as if he was trying to test the limits of the credulity of his interrogators. Perhaps he had not realised that they were supposed not to show any overt reaction to whatever they were told. If he had taken their apparent passivity for belief in what he said, it might be expected that there would eventually have been an 'April Fool!' moment of disclosure and merriment, but that never came. He certainly held a strong self-image up to this point, and wished to have his capabilities recognised, but he seemed not to be given to bravado.

Nevertheless, it must at least be considered that he could really have been trying to delude his captors. The only participant known to have suspected that was the senior RAF interrogator Wing Commander Denys Felkin. Welbourn records that Felkin started to wonder if Cleff had been deliberately planted to mislead them, or did so while playing them along for what he could get out of it. Providing a stream of new information might gain him some privileges, whilst still deceiving them, and if what he said was sufficiently novel its main effect might be to alarm his interviewers and not be enquired into too closely.

Felkin thought that a prisoner's point of view was always basically patriotic, embodied in the saying 'my country, right or wrong'. He was perhaps thinking of the example of his many RAF compatriots, now prisoners in Germany, who at least adhered firmly to the precept of giving only 'Name, Rank and Number' when interrogated. But most would take any opportunity to deceive the enemy if they could, whilst others pledged themselves never to cease trying to escape. Felkin wanted to press Cleff hard about his claims, but had been dissuaded by Welbourn, who thought that this would jeopardise the plan to get him to work for the British authorities. And so there was to be no opportunity to consider how he would react if his more exaggerated claims were being firmly challenged.

A somewhat similar conclusion to Felkin's was that reached by David Irving, who came across copies of the intelligence reports when researching for his book *The Mare's Nest*. He thought that having told his interrogators everything he knew about tanks and submarine propulsion, Cleff became like 'Scheherazade', fearful of the consequences if his flow of stories should dry up. And so he began to utilise his imagination, and had sensed that rocketry was a good field for that, although he was unlikely to have known that his timing was fortunate, due to 'the scare that was then reaching its climax within the War Cabinet'. He was also thought to have been clever in including the occasional factual items distributed throughout his statements, as these were often about things that were already known or could be readily verified, to give credence to the parts that were invented.

After the publication of Irving's views, Welbourn reacted strongly, complaining that he had obtained his information from reports which had been passed in confidence to the US Air Force, and in his book he had not merely got many of his facts wrong, but published a libellous account of Cleff's motives. This had also by-passed the directive, initialled by Churchill, that nothing about the actions concerning Cleff was to be divulged during his lifetime. In fact, Irving did not actually reveal his name, referring to him at first as 'Captain C----', although later he did go further by using his cover name of 'Mr Peter Herbert'. Welbourn showed a prejudice when asserting that for Irving, 'Hitler could do no wrong, and anyone who opposed him could do no right'. This was hindsight, based on the controversy over some of Irving's later writings, but there had been no trace of that opinion in this context.

Irving also noted how everyone who met Cleff 'soon fell under the spell of his charm'. He thought that it had been his youthful enthusiasm and apparent scientific capability that persuaded them to take him seriously, although he claimed that later they were to regret their trust in him. That could not be said about Welbourn however, who maintained his support for Cleff over many years. Whilst not being entirely blind to his faults, he usually muted his criticisms. Already at the first interrogation he attended, he perceived that 'he is apt to draw on his imagination when his knowledge of a subject is limited'. Later, Cleff had claimed, when talking about his early life, that after the first year of his studies in Berlin, he had paid his way there by having 'designed, patented and sold a novel type of governor'. Evidently wondering about that, Welbourn had looked for, but failed to find, any record of a patent in his name, but remarked mildly only that 'his imagination was sometimes curious'. His description of Cleff's information on high-speed U-boats was oddly ambiguous – it was 'firm but inexact'. Only when towards the end of his life Cleff called him to say that his gear-grinding machine was to be built in Germany, Welbourn had come to believe that by then fantasy had taken over completely, as if finally acknowledging that fantasy had always been present in him to some degree.

13.2 Envoi

The final question here is whether Cleff had simply lied to his captors when making his extravagant claims about advances in German technology. Basically, someone lies when he says something that is false. Pedants can insert a wedge into this definition by questioning whether it is lying to say something false, whilst not knowing at the time whether it is false or true. Philosophers debate the morality of the 'white lie', where we persuade ourselves that less harm is done by saying something false than by giving the truth, when this would cause distress or have the potential to start great mischief. A path must now be found through this maze to close the account.

There were two contemporary views. Felkin thought that Cleff was deliberately deceiving his interrogators, perhaps even having been planted for this purpose. If so, he had lied, on the basis of knowing at the time that what he said was false. But this was just what our own personnel were expected to do if captured, so would not be surprising. It would just mean that little weight should be placed on the testimony of prisoners in general. Welbourn believed however that Cleff's claims were honest projections of where the technology was likely to have reached, obtained by applying his scientific understanding to the state of things as he had seen or heard about them at times prior to his capture. This was not intended to be deceitful, but rather to help, by warning of potential threats, so that measures to meet them could be put in hand. With good intent, this was not lying, as he could not have known at the time whether or not things had worked out as he imagined. He was not to blame if the problems he addressed were 'solved differently'. Wiser counsel would have argued that Cleff should simply have made it clear whenever he was giving conjectural projections, and that it was at least mischievous not to have done so.

Felkin was the senior RAF interrogator at Latimer House, with enough experience to have felt that he had seen most sides of human nature. His intention was to press Cleff hard over details of his account, with the expectation that flaws in it would be exposed and challenged. Welbourn however had been seconded into interrogation because of his engineering background, which had been lacking in the RN team. He does not say that he received any training in the task before encountering Cleff, who was perhaps even his first case. At their first meeting, he had sat in with other Navy interrogators, and so, as in much other unfamiliar activity in wartime, he was probably expected to pick up the technique as he went along.

In recounting his efforts to nudge Cleff towards defection, he makes a point of mentioning that, whilst no longer a believer himself, he was still guided by the Christian values of the society in which he grew up. There are other instances in his memoirs of where he had looked for the best of intentions in others, and his approach to Cleff seems also to reflect that. But whatever his approach had been, Welbourn must have shown unusual powers of persuasion when as a newcomer Lieutenant he prevailed upon Felkin, the experienced Wing Commander team-leader, not to proceed with further interrogation. Through that, he had been able to build up the close personal acquaintance that had reinforced his confidence in Cleff's qualities, but in the process also spared him some potentially uncomfortable exposure.

Irving's assessment came some years afterwards, not through any direct contact, but through studying the interrogation reports. It was that Cleff was simply acting in self-interest. As long as he could come up with stories plausible enough to catch the attention of the intelligence services, he might receive privileges. Not the least of these was perhaps that of remaining longer as someone of interest and being held in the relative comfort of Latimer House, instead of being moved on to an undistinguished existence in an ordinary prison camp. It would be a bonus if his conjectures turned out to be near to the truth, but where they were falsely presented as recollections of his own experiences, the charge of lying could not then be dismissed.

Of these possibilities, Felkin's conclusion seems to be the least convincing. There was little in Cleff's testimony about developments in tank engineering that was not already known, or suspected from other sources. But that was the response to his first experience of interrogation, and he might have been wary of attempting deceit in that area.

Concerning marine propulsion, he seemed proud of the advanced turbine power plant that he and his colleagues had developed and that was probably just as he described it. He correctly reported also that surface vessels and submarines had been achieving unheard-of speeds, and that a new fuel was enabling submarines to run submerged on their main engines. Further, it was true that this fuel was being used in aircraft and missile propulsion, and had been considered for use as an explosive. But as to the nature of the fuel itself, it was likely that he had picked up only a few scattered fragments of information, on the basis of which he had made a conjecture as to its composition.

The experts who considered his account had assumed that it must have been a previously-unknown kind of hydrocarbon fuel, combined in some way with the necessary oxygen to render it autonomous. They had soon established from first principles that nothing of this nature could release anything like the energy quantities quoted by Cleff, and this part of his testimony was accordingly discredited comprehensively. However, it can now be seen that this 'fuel' was in fact hydrogen peroxide, and that it had been produced from a feedstock with a molecular structure containing three fused benzene rings, just as he had reported. It seems also that he had probably quoted correctly the energy figures that he had heard, although he had failed to realise that they had been given in molar units, and would need to be divided by a substantial figure for a valid comparison to be made with those for other fuels given in mass units. It was with some embarrassment that he acknowledged to G. I. Taylor that the figures he quoted seemed improbable. Accordingly, it seems fair to conclude that Cleff had made an understandable and innocent mistake, and had not lied about this part of his story either.

It was only when he came to his concluding testimony about aircraft and rockets that he had no personal experience to work on, and here it seems beyond question that he had resorted to his imagination. This later material was not significantly tested following Welbourn's intervention to secure the application of his talents to the British war effort. Only when comparisons could be made with the real situation, as revealed after the war, could it be certain that most of his claims in these areas were inventions. Although some doubts about them had been recorded within the interrogation reports themselves, and a moment's further reflection should have been sufficient to show that much of the story was questionable, the small staff at Latimer had much else to do. It was probably thought that anything further concerning Cleff was now down to Welbourn to follow up. His later conclusion was that Cleff had merely exercised his imagination to envisage the current state of things about which he had heard or read at earlier times, but it had at least been deceitful not to make this clear whenever that was the case, and to represent some occurrences as having been within his own experience. When, for example, he had claimed to have been shown photographs of aircraft, which were later found to have been non-existent, the conclusion that he had finally resorted to lying becomes inescapable.

It was essentially Welbourn's actions that settled the outcome. Once he had obtained Cleff's agreement to collaborate he immediately began to seek a suitable occupation for him. And there, it could be said that Welbourn's confidence in him was vindicated, in that he acquitted himself sufficiently well to move on later to the full life as a British citizen that is described here.

Nevertheless, it is probably Irving's assessment that best fits the facts about Cleff's motivation as they are known, over the whole period from his capture until the time he was released into civilian life. From his first interrogation in Egypt he related more about his life history and his role in the Army than was usual, suggesting that he wanted to make sure that his capabilities were recognised and respected. His claim to have heard about a secret new weapon that was too frightful to contemplate was not mentioned again after that. He had said that he would never divulge what he knew anyway, so perhaps this was brought in to bolster his own self-image. At Latimer House, he was probably flattered by the unusual attention he received from Welbourn, and the visits during which he was taken outside the centre, hard to believe for a prisoner-of-war, had certainly done that. These had included one to view Churchill tanks in production and on another occasion being taken to lunch with the legendary engine expert Harry Ricardo, a heroic figure to Cleff.

In his first reports he had no need to depart significantly from the facts, as they showed that he had an unusually wide range of experiences for someone just over 30, serving to enhance his standing. Then, when he no longer had subjects that he could describe from personal experience, he began to construct stories that he thought were plausible. To this, he could bring to bear a considerable intellect and a broad acquaintance with scientific principles.

Although now having to talk of technical areas of which he had no direct knowledge, he sought to construct situations which might reasonably be extrapolated from those that he had heard about before his capture, and perhaps some that had been spoken of by fellow-prisoners. When he had to deal with the new fuel, he reported correctly what he had heard. But whatever he might have learned about the chemistry of combustion during his diploma course lay too far in the past and he failed to recognise the need for a change of units when quoting the energy values. This led to his account being dismissed, perhaps unfairly, but by then he had built up enough trust, especially with Welbourn's active support, for the rest of his testimony not to be discredited entirely.

The ultimate judgment of his claims about long-range rockets would fall to someone outside the interrogation centre, like R. V. Jones, who had to weigh up a great many reports from a wide rage of sources. His account came at a time when Jones was already distrusting other stories of missiles up to 100 tons in weight, and so it was probably not given much credence. The greatest risk of exposure should have come from the Supersonics Committee, but there he was fortunate to have another uncritical supporter in the influential figure of Frank Whittle. Even in the pre-war years, Whittle had voiced his belief that supersonic flight was entirely feasible, and now, after his long advocacy of jet propulsion had been vindicated, his standing was such that his opinion would be hard to discount. Such doubts as there were about the credibility of Cleff's evidence became submerged in anxiety that the enemy might have made a spectacular advance in an area that had been overlooked by the Allies.

And so, just as he had been likened by Irving to Scheherazade, when his stories ran out, Cleff was saved by being valued for himself, rather than for the tales he had to tell. He had been moved out of danger of exposure by his appointments at the Ministry of Supply and the Admiralty, where his engineering work was evidently appreciated sufficiently to ensure his continued employment there, even at the time of retrenchment after the war. His feverish activity during this time could have been due mainly to the trait in his personality of a need to have his capabilities recognised, which had been noted from the earliest days of his capture. This would be reinforced by a natural compulsion to maintain the favoured position in which he found himself. Speculative story-telling was no longer enough; now it was necessary to produce real results on a regular basis, and seemingly by hard application he was able to do that.

In this and his later work, Cleff proved that he had the skills to build a successful professional life, but his legacy is difficult to evaluate. Contributions he made while in government service remain largely hidden. His long series of patents on gear-grinding and inspection machines, although ingenious, seem never to have resulted in actual applications. Potentially the most momentous consequence of his presence in Britain would have been the successful completion of the Miles M.52 supersonic aircraft, but because of its security rating of Most Secret, the existence of this project was known only to a very small circle of people. When the first information about it finally began to emerge in the autumn of 1946, comments expressing indignation over its abrupt cancellation appeared in the newspapers and technical journals. But even if he read some of those, Cleff would probably not have suspected that the project had any connection with something he had said at Latimer more than three years before. Nor did Irving or Welbourn record anything to indicate that they had realised this either. Yet if the Miles aircraft had been completed as planned and become the first in the world to fly faster than sound, that would have been because a conjecture by this German prisoner-of-war, who was really a tank expert, had been accepted uncritically – truly a flight of fancy.

Acknowledgments

Permission to quote material from the following for inclusion in the text is gratefully acknowledged :

Margaret Hardy, for D. B. Welbourn, *An Engineer in Peace and War*, Vols I & II, Lulu, 2008, ISBN 978-1-84799-694-7 & 978-1-84799-695-4, and Vol III, CD

David Irving, for David Irving, *The Mare's Nest*, William Kimber & Co Ltd, London, UK, 1964

Penguin Books Ltd for R. V. Jones, *Most Secret War*, Hamish Hamilton Ltd, London, UK, 1978, p342

The National Archives, Kew, Richmond, Surrey, UK, for numerous documents under Crown Copyright, principally WO 208/3464 *Hauptmann Herbert Cleff* and AVIA 15/1908 *Athodyd propulsion for aircraft flying at supersonic speeds*

Peter Amos, for material from the Miles Aircraft Collection

Brian Riddle, Librarian of the Royal Aeronautical Society, for help in locating documents in The National Aerospace Library, Farnborough

Valuable assistance was received also from staff at
The International Committee of the Red Cross, Geneva, Switzerland
The Federal Archives, Department of Military Archives, Freiburg, Germany
The German Military Service Centre, Berlin, Germany
Companies House, Cardiff, Wales, UK
The Intellectual Property Office, London, UK
The Museum of Science & Industry, Collections Dept, Manchester, UK
The Identity & Passport Service, General Register Office, Southport, UK
The Coroner's Office, Newcastle upon Tyne, UK

It is pleasing to recall friendship and encouragement during the preparation of this book from Elizabeth and Dennis Bancroft and Peter Amos.

Index